YOU CAN MAKE IT FOR CAMP AND COTTAGE

PRACTICAL RUSTIC WOODWORKING PROJECTS,
CABIN FURNITURE, AND ACCESSORIES
FROM RECLAIMED WOOD

BY **U.S. DEPARTMENT OF COMMERCE
NATIONAL COMMITTEE ON WOOD
UTILIZATION**

ORIGINALLY PUBLISHED IN 1930

LEGACY EDITION

THE DOUBLEBIT
CABIN LIFE AND CABIN CRAFT COLLECTION
BOOK 7

Doublebit Press
Eugene. OR

New content, introduction, and annotations
Copyright © 2020 by Doublebit Press. All rights reserved.

Doublebit Press is an imprint of Eagle Nest Press
www.doublebitpress.com | Eugene, OR, USA

Original content under the public domain. Originally published in 1930 by the U.S. Department of Commerce, National Committee on Wood Utilization, Subcommittee on Camp and Cottage Equipment.

This title and other Doublebit Press books are available at a volume discount for youth groups, outdoors clubs, or reading groups. Contact at info@doublebitpress.com for more information.

Doublebit Press Legacy Edition ISBNs
Hardcover: 978-1-64389-135-4
Paperback: 978-1-64389-136-1

Disclaimer: Because of its age and historic context, this text could contain content on present-day inappropriate methods, activities, outdated medical information, unsafe chemical and mechanical processes, or culturally and racially insensitive content. Doublebit Press, or its employees, authors, and other affiliates, assume no liability for any actions performed by readers or any damages that might be related to information contained in this book. This text has been published for historical study and for personal literary enrichment toward the goal of preserving the American handcraft tradition, timeless trade skills, and traditional artisanal knowledge.

First Doublebit Press Legacy Edition Printing, 2020

Printed in the United States of America
when purchased at retail in the USA

INTRODUCTION
To The Doublebit Press Legacy Edition

The old experts of artisanal trades, country and homestead knowledge, and the woods and mountains taught timeless principles and skills for centuries. Through their timeless books, the old experts offered rich descriptions of how the world works and encouraged learning through personal experiences *by doing*. Over the last 125 years, manufacturing, farming, and construction have substantially changed. Of course, many things have gotten simpler as equipment and technology have improved. In addition, some activities of pre-digital times are now no longer in vogue, or are even outright considered inappropriate or illegal. However, despite many of the positive changes in manufacturing and crafting methods that have occurred over the years, *there are many other skills and much knowledge that have been forgotten.*

By publishing *Doublebit Legacy Editions*, it is our goal at Doublebit Press to do what we can to preserve and share the works from forgotten teachers that form the cornerstone of the history of the American artisans and traditional crafts. Through remastered reprint editions of timeless classics, perhaps we can regain some of this lost knowledge for future generations.

This book is an important contribution traditional handcraft and country skills literature and has important historical and collector value toward preserving the American handcraft and outdoors tradition. The knowledge it holds is an invaluable reference for practicing skills and hand craft methods. Its chapters thoroughly discuss some of the essential building blocks of knowledge that are fundamental but may have been forgotten as equipment gets fancier and technology gets smarter. In short, this book was chosen for Legacy Edition printing because much of the basic skills and knowledge it contains has been forgotten or put to the wayside in trade for more modern conveniences and methods.

With technology playing a major role in everyday life, sometimes we need to take a step back in time to find those basic building blocks used for gaining mastery – the things that we have luckily not completely lost and has been recorded in books over the last two centuries. These skills aren't forgotten, they've just been shelved. *It's time to unshelve them once again and reclaim the lost knowledge of self-sufficiency.*

Based on this commitment to preserving our outdoors and handcraft artisanal heritage, we have taken great pride in publishing this book as a complete original work. We hope it is worthy of both study and collection by outdoors folk in the modern era of outdoors and traditional skills life.

Unlike many other photocopy reproductions of classic books that are common on the market, this Legacy Edition does not simply place poor photography of old texts on our pages and use error-prone optical scanning or computer-generated text. We want our work to speak for itself, and reflect the quality demanded by our customers who spend their hard-earned money. With this in mind, each Legacy Edition book that has been chosen for publication is carefully remastered from original print books, *with the Doublebit Legacy Edition printed and laid out in the exact way that it was presented at its original publication.* We provide a beautiful, memorable experience that is as true to the original text as best as possible, but with the aid of modern technology to make as beautiful a reading experience as possible for books that can be over a century old.

Because of its age and because it is presented in its original form, the book may contain misspellings, inking errors from print plates, and other printing blemishes that were common for the age. However, these are exactly the things that we feel give the book its character, which we preserved in this Legacy Edition. During digitization, we ensured that each illustration in the text was clean and sharp with the least amount of loss from being copied and digitized as possible. Full-page plate illustrations are presented as they were found, often including the extra blank page that was often behind a plate. For the covers, we use the original cover design to give the book its original feel. We are sure you'll appreciate the fine touches and attention to detail that your Legacy Edition has to offer.

For traditional handcrafters and classic artisanal enthusiasts who demand the best from their equipment, this Doublebit Press Legacy Edition reprint was made with you in mind. Both important and minor details have equally both been accounted for by our publishing staff, down to the cover, font, layout, and images. It is the goal of Doublebit Legacy Edition series to be worthy of collection in any outdoorsperson's library and that can be passed to future generations.

Every book selected to be in this series offers unique views and instruction on important skills, advice, tips, tidbits, anecdotes, stories, and experiences that will enrich the repertoire of any person who enjoys escaping a bit from today's modern technology-based, cookie-cutter, and highly industrialized skills. Instead, folks seeking to make things with their hands like the old days may find great value from these resurrected instructional manuals from the past. These books were not simply written to be shelved in a library – they contain our history and forgotten methods to make things with real character and energy with a *human* component.

Therefore, to learn the most basic building blocks of a craft leads to mastery of all its aspects. We hope this book helps you along this path with its rich descriptions and illustrations!

U. S. DEPARTMENT OF COMMERCE
WOOD UTILIZATION

YOU CAN MAKE IT
FOR
CAMP AND COTTAGE

NATIONAL COMMITTEE ON WOOD UTILIZATION
SUBCOMMITTEE ON CAMP AND COTTAGE EQUIPMENT

ASSISTANCE GIVEN BY THE DEPARTMENT OF COMMERCE TO FOREST INDUSTRIES

The National Committee on Wood Utilization is receiving valuable aid from the bureaus and divisions of the Department of Commerce wholly or partly engaged in promoting the interests of our forest and wood-using industries.

Bureau of the Census.

This bureau is in charge of the compilation of statistical material covering a great variety of topics. It is closely cooperating with the committee in furnishing statistical data concerning forest industries and the consumption of forest products.

Division of agriculture.—This division compiles, in connection with the quinquennial census of agriculture, a variety of information regarding the acreage, burnings, clearings, and production of farm woodland.

Division of manufacture.—This division compiles, in connection with the biennial census of manufacture, data on the manufacturing industries of the United States, including the basic forest-products industries and the wood-reworking industries.

Bureau of Foreign and Domestic Commerce.

This bureau is directly engaged in promoting the foreign and domestic trade of the United States. Through it American business organizations are receiving assistance in acquiring new business and in furthering trade already established. The bureau maintains 29 district and 50 cooperative offices in the United States and 56 offices in the principal foreign trade centers.

Lumber division.—This division was organized to assist export trade in lumber and lumber products. It also studies various problems affecting the lumber trade of the United States. The National Committee on Wood Utilization is extending good wood-using practices in the foreign field with the assistance of this division.

Paper division.—This division is engaged in promoting the interests of American pulp and paper manufacturers in the foreign and domestic fields.

Chemical division.—The chemical division promotes the sale of American chemicals and allied products in foreign markets and gives information and statistical service, conducts market surveys, and cooperates with the manufacturers of wood chemicals and other chemical products. It is closely cooperating with the committee in wood chemical studies in the United States and abroad.

Domestic commerce division.—This division includes among its activities the national regional market surveys, the national retail credit survey, the industrial capacity and distributive practices survey, distribution cost studies, and regional commodity movement studies. The division also compiles information as to activities in market research, trade associations, and industrial and commercial organizations. It maintains a special inquiry service and provides current information and assistance through the bureau's weekly pamphlet Domestic Commerce.

Bureau of Standards.

The Bureau of Standards is cooperating with 200 scientific, technical, and industrial organizations. It operates the largest scientific laboratory in the world.

Division of simplified practice.—This division is engaged largely in the standardization and simplification of forest products. The committee is closely cooperating with this division in extending good wood-using practices in the consumer's field.

Division of building and housing.—The work of this division is mainly devoted to the promotion of better practices in building and construction fields. A notable improvement has been made in building code work. Since building and construction offer the largest outlet for forest products, the committee's work is closely connected with this division.

Bureau of Mines.

One of the major activities of the Bureau of Mines has to do with increased safety, efficiency, and economic development in mining, and with the conservation of our mineral resources. The mining industry is one of the largest consumers of forest products, and for that reason the committee has established close relations with this bureau.

The committee is also receiving aid from other bureaus of the Department of Commerce, such as the Bureau of Fisheries, Bureau of Lighthouses, Coast and Geodetic Survey, Bureau of Navigation, Steamboat Inspection Service, and Bureau of Patents.

U. S. DEPARTMENT OF COMMERCE
WOOD UTILIZATION

YOU CAN MAKE IT
FOR
CAMP AND COTTAGE
PRACTICAL USES FOR SECONDHAND WOODEN CONTAINERS AND ODD PIECES OF LUMBER

[Volume II of "You Can Make It" Series]

Report of the
Subcommittee on Camp and Cottage Equipment
of the
NATIONAL COMMITTEE ON WOOD UTILIZATION

(Sixteenth report of a series on the marketing and use of lumber)

UNITED STATES
GOVERNMENT PRINTING OFFICE
WASHINGTON : 1930

For sale by the Superintendent of Documents, U. S. Government Printing Office
Washington 25, D. C.
Price 20 cents

PUBLICATIONS OF THE NATIONAL COMMITTEE ON WOOD UTILIZATION

THE MARKETING OF SHORT-LENGTH LUMBER.

This report contains a careful analysis of more than 250 house plans representing the typical small American house and shows that about 20 per cent of the total lumber bill may be purchased in lengths of less than 8 feet, while in actual practice only about 1½ per cent of the lumber is bought in short lengths, the balance (18½ per cent) being cut into short lengths from long lengths on the job. Tables show where these short lengths may be used in building and construction. Price, 5 cents per copy.

END-MATCHED SOFTWOOD LUMBER AND ITS USES.

A discussion of the manufacture of end-matched softwood lumber, its handling, storing, and use, with particular reference to building and construction. The report points out an important saving in the use of lumber and installation costs. Price, 5 cents per copy.

SAWDUST AND WOOD FLOUR.

This report gives a detailed description of the known uses of sawdust, together with a description of how this material should be treated and handled. The subject of wood flour (ground sawdust) is given special treatment, mainly with the idea of making the United States independent of foreign supplies of this material. Price, 10 cents per copy.

GRADE MARKING OF LUMBER FOR THE CONSUMERS' PROTECTION.

This bulletin explains grade marking as applied to lumber and shows the benefits and economies of specifying and using lumber marked to indicate quality. Price, 5 cents per copy.

SEASONING, HANDLING, AND CARE OF LUMBER (Consumers' Edition).

First of a series of four monographs on the proper seasoning, handling, and care of lumber. Written from the consumer's point of view. Price, 10 cents per copy.

SEASONING, HANDLING, AND CARE OF LUMBER (Distributors' Edition).

The second of a series of four monographs on the proper seasoning, handling, and care of lumber. Written from the distributor's point of view. Price, 10 cents per copy.

SEASONING, HANDLING, AND CARE OF LUMBER (Fabricators' Edition).

The third of a series of four monographs on the proper seasoning, handling, and care of lumber. Written from the fabricator's point of view. Price, 10 cents per copy.

SURVEY OF NONUTILIZED WOOD IN VIRGINIA.

The first of a series of State surveys of nonutilized wood occurring at sawmills and wood-fabricating plants. Methods of utilizing and disposing of wood waste are suggested, together with recognized practices which decrease waste production. An appendix lists the name and address of each firm which has nonutilized wood for disposal as well as the kind, amount, and species of this material. A large map folder shows the distribution of waste by counties and the location of each mill which has reported nonutilized wood. Price, 20 cents per copy.

SEASONING, HANDLING, AND CARE OF LUMBER (Manufacturers' Edition).

Last of a series of four monographs on the seasoning, handling, and care of lumber. Written from the lumber producer's point of view. Price, 10 cents per copy.

THE SAP STAINS OF WOOD AND THEIR PREVENTION.

A detailed discussion of sap stains and their prevention. It describes types and kinds of fungi, means of identifying and treatments, with types of equipment and layout of machinery for chemical treatment of lumber for the prevention of sap stain. Price, 10 cents per copy.

The above publications are for sale by the Superintendent of Documents, Government Printing Office, Washington, D. C. Special rates for purchase in quantity will be furnished on application.

CONTENTS

	Page
Publications of the National Committee on Wood Utilization	II
National Committee on Wood Utilization	V
Subcommittee on camp and cottage equipment	V
Foreword	VI
General instructions:	1
Sources of material	1
Tools	1
Preparing the material for use	1
Decorating the finished article	1
Part I. Outdoors	3–20
Part II. Indoors	21–38
Appendix:	38–47
Prevent forest fires	38
Appendix—Continued.	
Attracting birds	39
Dimensions and locations of bird houses	40
Woodworking tools commonly used	41
Hardware frequently used	42
Cooperage	43
Fruit and vegetable packages	43
Plywood boxes make useful articles	44
Nailed wooden boxes	45
How to reclaim the lumber in wire-bound boxes	46
American Lumber Standards	47
Bibliography	47
Index	48
Contents of Volume I	49

ILLUSTRATIONS

Fig.		Page
1.	Aquaplane	3
2.	Canoe lazyback	3
3.	Live bait box	4
4.	Fishing tackle box	5
5.	Rabbit trap	6
6.	Water turtle trap	6
7.	Chickadee, titmouse, or nuthatch house	6
8.	Bluebird house	7
9.	Wren house	7
10.	Flicker house	7
11.	Barn-owl house	7
12.	Robin, catbird, or brown thrasher shelter	8
13.	Swallow or phœbe nest shelf	8
14.	Song sparrow shelter	8
15.	Finch house	8
16.	Bird feed box	8
17.	Bird feeding house (revolving)	9
18.	Mail box	9
19.	Iceless refrigerator	10
20.	Garden stick	11
21.	Door knocker	11
22.	Barrel-stave hammock	12
23.	Folding table top	12
24.	Table horse	13
25.	Folding table	13
26.	Weather vane	14
27.	Shower	14
28.	Hurdle	14
29.	Stile	14
30.	Bean-bag target	15
31.	Dart target	15
32.	Auto jack	15
33.	Tent peg	15
34.	Beach sandal	16
35.	Sign	16
36.	Foot scraper	16
37.	Sawbuck	17
38.	Spring refrigerator	18
39.	Salt box (animals)	18
40.	Clothesline reel	18
41.	Lighthouse	18
42.	Ore boat	19
43.	Canal boat	19
44.	Steamboat	19
45.	Tugboat	20
46.	Scow	20
47.	Folding dressing table	21
48.	Rocker	21
49.	Vanity	22
50.	Vanity bench	22
51.	Bootery	23
52.	Ventilator	23
53.	Linen closet	24
54.	Book and magazine rack	24
55.	Waste-paper basket	24
56.	Desk set	24
57.	Desk bookcase	25
58.	Correspondence holder	25
59.	Adjustable book ends	25
60.	Desk	26
61.	Typewriter stand	26
62.	Reading table	26
63.	Bookcase seat	27
64.	Tabouret	27
65.	Drop-leaf table	27

CONTENTS

Fig.		Page
66.	Coat and hat rack	28
67.	Chair	28
68.	Sconce	28
69.	Fireplace wood basket	28
70.	Desk filing cabinet	29
71.	Shelf	30
72.	Window seat	30
73.	Bracket	31
74.	Breakfast table and cabinet	31
75.	Window flytrap	31
76.	Knife, fork, and spoon tray	32
77.	Elevated wood box	33
78.	Trash receptacle	33
79.	Pan lid rack	33
80.	Towel rack	33
81.	Clothes drier	34
82.	Stool	34
83.	Clotheshorse	34
84.	Safety-match box holder	34
85.	Broom holder	35
86.	Bench	35
87.	Kitchen table	35
88.	Wall plate rack	35
89.	Meat or bread board	36
90.	Fishing pole rack	36
91.	Tool chest	36
92.	Bathroom cabinet	37
93.	First-aid box	37
94.	Portable tool box	37
95.	Head mounting board	37
96.	Bootjack	38
97.	Necktie rack	38
98.	Camp fire correctly built	39
99.	Camp fire correctly extinguished	39

NATIONAL COMMITTEE ON WOOD UTILIZATION

R. P. LAMONT, Secretary of Commerce, chairman.
R. Y. STUART, Forester, United States Forest Service, Department of Agriculture, vice chairman.
AXEL H. OXHOLM, director.

The National Committee on Wood Utilization, organized by Herbert Hoover, as Secretary of Commerce, comprises about 200 members, representing manufacturers, distributors, and consumers of forest products. Its object is to work for closer utilization of our country's timber resources. The committee, whose headquarters are in the Department of Commerce, Washington, D. C., works in close cooperation with a number of official and private organizations, notably the Bureau of Standards of the Department of Commerce and the Forest Products Laboratory of the Forest Service, Department of Agriculture.

SUBCOMMITTEE ON CAMP AND COTTAGE EQUIPMENT

WALTER JOHNSON, president, Tarter, Webster & Johnson, San Francisco, Calif., chairman.
RALPH TAYLOR, president, Jamestown Table Co., Jamestown, N. Y.
C. C. COOK, maintenance engineer, the Baltimore & Ohio Railroad, Baltimore, Md.
U. M. CARLTON, treasurer, Dix Lumber Co., North Cambridge, Mass.
FRANK G. WISNER, treasurer, Eastman, Gardiner & Co., Laurel, Miss.
RAY M. HUDSON, industrial executive, New England Council, Boston, Mass.
M. S. WINDER, executive secretary, American Farm Bureau Federation, Chicago, Ill.
H. L. PEASE, secretary-manager, Plywood Box Manufacturers of America, Boston, Mass.

FOREWORD

The National Committee on Wood Utilization was organized for the purpose of increasing a knowledge of the correct uses of wood.

We are told that approximately 4,000,000,000 feet of lumber is used each year in the construction of wooden containers. Once these containers have served their original purpose they are usually thrown away or otherwise wasted. If it were possible to use this lumber for construction purposes, about 400,000 average-size frame houses could be erected—enough to shelter a population four times that of the Nation's capital. Millions of feet of odd pieces of lumber are also being wasted. This material can be and is being applied to the making of useful articles, as shown in Volume I of the committee's You Can Make It series of booklets on the subject of uses for wooden container material and odd pieces of lumber.

The wide-spread popularity of Volume I of the committee's You Can Make It series is shown by the fact that over 150,000 copies have been sold in less than a year. As a result of the demand for Volume I and for additional booklets of this series, the committee has prepared this, the second volume of the series of booklets on the subject of uses for wooden-container material and odd pieces of lumber.

The making of the simple devices illustrated in these booklets should give boys and girls an elementary knowledge of the essential points of wood construction in its various applications, which will stand them in good stead later on in life. Such work will also develop self-reliance and practical sense.

These pamphlets have been prepared by H. Conrad Hoover, of the committee staff, for special subcommittees interested in waste elimination who are sponsoring the series.

The committee desires to express its appreciation of the valuable assistance given by the Playground and Recreation Association of America, Boys' Club Federation, Boy Scouts of America, and the Y. M. C. A. Grateful acknowledgement is also made of assistance rendered by the office of the Superintendent of Prisons, the Department of Justice, and the Bureau of Foreign and Domestic Commerce of the Department of Commerce, in the preparation of drawings. Valuable assistance was also received from Dr. H. A. Gardner, who prepared the text on decorating the finished article.

The material in the book is based partly on original ideas and partly on information from both domestic and foreign sources. In each case credit has been given where credit is due.

The committee hopes that these booklets will be instrumental in teaching boys and girls the proper use of wood, and will induce them to make their own toys and equipment. The booklet will also be of interest to manual training teachers, vocational directors, and playground directors.

AXEL H. OXHOLM, Director.

JUNE 2, 1930.

YOU CAN MAKE IT

For Camp and Cottage

GENERAL INSTRUCTIONS

SOURCES OF MATERIAL

Grocery, hardware, or department stores and most other commercial establishments have a constant supply of wooden containers of which they are usually glad to dispose at little or no cost. Also, in many lumberyards one may secure odd pieces of lumber at lower cost than regular yard items.

Since the lumber needed is all less than 8 feet in length, no difficulty will be found in transporting it. In some cases it may be feasible for several boys to cart away the containers by wagonloads, as storekeepers generally do not like to be bothered with the handing out of one or two containers at a time. In other instances the material may be carried in the car or on the running board.

TOOLS

If one desires a fairly complete outfit of tools, the following list will serve as a guide:

1 claw hammer, 13-ounce.
1 screw driver, 4-inch.
1 two-foot folding rule.
1 crosscut saw, 22-inch.
1 try and miter square, 6-inch.
2 chisels, ¼ and ¾ inch.

1 marking gage.
1 jack plane, 11½-inch.
1 ratchet brace, 8-inch sweep.
2 auger bits, ⅜ and ¾ inch.
1 oilstone.
1 jackknife.

PREPARING THE MATERIAL FOR USE

Use of sandpaper and a plane will remove markings stenciled on the containers as well as scratches and other defacing marks, or it may be desirable to remove marred boards and nail them back in place with the marred surfaces inside. If a nail puller is not available, the sides and bottoms of the containers may easily be removed from the ends by hammering on a block of wood placed across the pieces to be removed as near the nailed sections as the inside of the containers will permit. This will eliminate splitting of the pieces.

The dimensions specified are suggested only to give some idea of the correct proportions of the article, and sizes that are slightly larger or smaller will serve the purpose as well.

DECORATING THE FINISHED ARTICLE

It is probable that the majority of articles outlined in this pamphlet will be prepared from old wooden containers which are made of softwoods. After the article has been completed and is ready for decoration it should be finished with attractive colors. Since most of these articles will be for interior use, it is not necessary that linseed-oil paints be applied. The latter type of paint is used on dwellings and is usually the most durable on wooden surfaces. Such paints are rather slow-drying in character as compared to varnish paints and lacquers. The latter two materials are now widely used for interior-decoration purposes, and would be entirely satisfactory for objects made from shipping container lumber.

Linseed-oil paints for exterior use may require 12 to 14 hours to become sufficiently dry so that a second coat may be applied. For interior work, lacquer usually dries so that the surface may be recoated in a period of about 30 minutes, although a slightly longer time is usually preferred. Color varnishes of the 4-hour type and clear varnishes of the same type dry in approximately 4 hours, but it is desirable to allow them 6 hours before recoating. The time will depend upon the season of the year and the ventilation in the place where the work is done. Varnish stains are combinations of a varnish with a staining material, which stain and varnish the wood in one operation. Beautiful effects may be obtained with mahogany varnish stains. Two coats are usually sufficient over a primed surface.

If there is no particular desire to have the object finished exceptionally well, varnish or lacquer products in clear or pigmented form may be applied in two or three coats without any priming of the surfaces.

If any exceptionally smooth and highly finished surface is desired, the cracks in the object should be filled with putty or crack filler, which may be purchased from any paint store. The whole surface could then be given a priming coat of silica wood filler, which may be purchased in liquid form at a paint store. After the primer has been allowed a sufficient period of time to become thoroughly hard and dry, varnish stain, color lacquer, or color varnish may be applied in one or two coats to obtain the desired finish. If the woodwork has any large number of knots present it is often desirable to touch up the knots with a coat of shellac. After drying, the finishing coats of colored product may be applied. After the first coat of color varnish or lacquer has been applied and allowed to thoroughly dry, it may be lightly rubbed with fine sandpaper to remove any imperfections before applying the final coat. A much smoother surface is thus obtained. Aluminum paint is sometimes used for touching up knots if the finishing coats are to be of paint for exterior surfaces. Highly satisfactory results are obtained with this treatment.

Lacquering or painting work should be done in a place where there is good ventilation and where there are no flames. The brushes used for lacquer should not be used for paint, varnish, or enamels. Lacquer brushes should be softened in lacquer solvent and kept well cleaned. Paint brushes should be washed in turpentine, thoroughly dried, and kept clean for the next operation.

Since many different colors may be desired on the objects to be finished, it would probably be desirable to purchase the products in pint or quart cans. If the colors obtainable at a paint store are not exactly those desired, two colors may be mixed together to produce different shades or tints.

Part I. OUTDOORS

AQUAPLANE

One piece 1⅝ by 20½ by 52 inches for *A*. Three pieces ²⁵⁄₃₂ by 1¾ by 20½ inches for cleats *B*. Brass flathead wood screws.

CANOE LAZYBACK

Eight pieces ⁷⁄₁₆ by 1⅝ by 28 inches for slats *A*. Two pieces ⁷⁄₁₆ by 1⅝ by 14 inches for cleats *B*. Nail slats *A* to cleats *B* as shown in Figure 2.

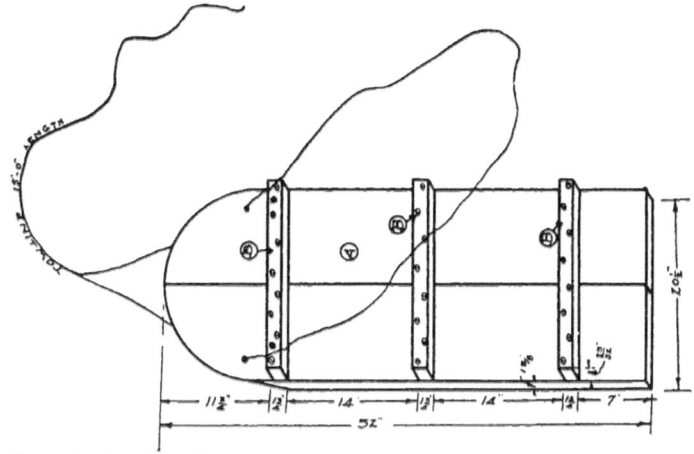

FIGURE 1.—*Aquaplane.*—If you can get a motor boat to tow you, by all means make and ride this plane

It may be necessary to use two or three planks to build the aquaplane *A*; if so, foot cleats *B* will hold them together securely. Fasten cleats *B* to planks *A* as shown in Figure 1, with brass wood screws. Round front end of aquaplane and bevel the under edge, as shown. Two holes are bored through the front cleat and the planks, for the towline, the ends of which are inserted through the bottom; knots in the ends will hold the line in place. Two other holes are bored through the planks about 3 inches in front of the front cleat, for the other rope, which the rider of the aquaplane holds. The towline is secured to a speed boat.

Then measure 24 inches along the outer edge of the outside slats. Mark an arc and cut the top ends of the slats along the arc, as shown.

LIVE-BAIT BOX

One box 20 by 15 by 12 inches. Four screw eyes. Rope or wire. Rustless wire screening.

Dismantle the box completely, leaving ends *D* intact. From the sides, top, and bottom cut pieces *A*, *B*, and *C*. (See fig. 3.) Cut the wire screening and secure it to ends *D* and strips *A* as they are nailed to *D*. Cut out the handhole in *B* and nail *B*

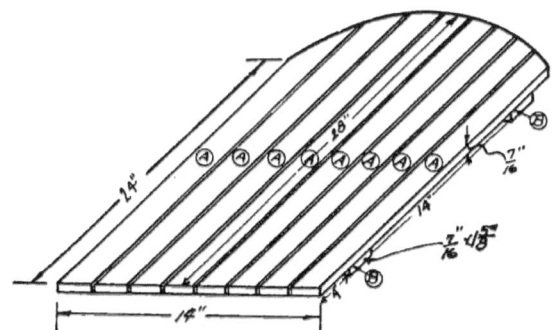

FIGURE 2.—*Canoe Lazyback.*—This requires little work but adds much to the comfort of the user

to top strips *A*. Secure the screw eyes in each of the four corners of the box, for wire or rope to attach box to boat while fishing.

FISHING-TACKLE BOX

Two pieces 5/16 by 5 9/16 by 20 3/4 inches for sides *A*. Two pieces 7/16 by 5 3/8 by 5 9/16 inches for ends *B*. Two pieces 7/16 by 6 by 20 3/4 inches for bottom and top *C*. Two pieces 5/16 by 1 1/16 by 20 3/4 inches for lid sides *D*. Two pieces 7/16 by 1 1/16 by 5 3/4 inches for lid ends *E*. Two pieces 5/16 by 1/2 inch for cleats *F*, one 5 3/8 inches long and the other 21 1/16 inches in length. Two pieces 3/16 by 2 1/2 by 3 1/16 inches for *G*. One piece 3/16 by 3 1/16 by 10 inches for *H*. Four pieces 5/16 by 1 7/16 by 19 7/8 inches for tray sides *I*. Four pieces 5/16 by 1 7/16 by 4 3/4 inches for tray ends *J*. Two pieces 5/16 by 5 3/8 by 19 7/8 inches for tray bottoms *K*. Five pieces 3/16 by 1 7/16 by 4 3/4 for tray partitions *L*. Five pieces 3/16 by 1 7/16 by 2 1/4 inches for tray partitions *M*. One piece 3/16 by 1 7/16 by 19 1/4 inches for tray partition *N*. Two butts (hinges).

Construct box by nailing sides *A*, ends *B*, and bottom *C* together, as shown in Figure 4. Construct lid by nailing sides *D*, ends *E*, and top *C* together. Nail cleats *F* to ends *B*. Nail pieces *G* and *H* together to form pockets in bottom of box, as shown. Bottom tray is constructed by nailing sides *I*, ends *J*, bottom *K*, and five partitions *L* together as shown. Top tray is constructed by nailing sides *I*, ends *J*, bottom *K*, and five partitions *M* and 1 partition *N* together as shown. Hinge lid to box. Trays rest on top of each other in box on top of cleats *F* and pockets in bottom.

RABBIT TRAP

One box *A*, almost any size. One box end for door *B*. Two pieces 7/16 by 1 1/4 inches for cleats *C*. Two pieces 7/16 by 7/8 inch for cleats *D*. One wooden barrel hoop *F*. Two sticks *E* and *G*. String.

Remove end from box *A*. The top of the box is shortened an amount equal to the thickness of the end of the box. Cleats *C* are nailed to the ends of the sides, while cleats *D* are nailed to the inside of the sides so as to form a track in which the end should slide easily, as shown in Figure 5. Bore hole through the top about 3 inches from the closed end of the box, through which stick *G* passes. *G* is notched and pointed as shown. Stick *E* is held loosely on top of hoop *F* by a staple driven into *F*.

As shown, door *B* is tied to one end of *E*, while stick *G* is tied to the other end. The notch in *G* placed against the rim of the hole holds the door up. An apple, lettuce, or some other food is attached to the pointed end of *G*. The rabbit enters the box, nibbles at the food, disengaging stick *G* which allows door *B* to drop, trapping the rabbit.

WATER-TURTLE TRAP

One box 12 by 14 by 24 inches *A*. One piece, thickness of box end by 10 inches by inside width of box for door *B*. One pair butts (hinges).

Remove one end of box. Nail a piece of the end about 1 1/2 inches wide back in place as shown by *C* in Figure 6. Hinge *B* to *C* so that its bottom edge rests on the bottom of the box. *B* will then be free to swing inward but not all the way outward.

The trap is weighted down with stones in a pond or stream where turtles are known to be. Scraps of meat placed inside the box will attract the turtles. After entering, they can not get out.

CHICKADEE, TITMOUSE, OR NUTHATCH HOUSE

Two pieces 11/16 by 5 5/8 by 8 1/8 inches for sides *A*. One piece 11/16 by 5 3/8 by 6 3/4 inches for *B*. One piece 11/16 by 5 3/8 by 7 1/2 inches for *C*. One piece 11/16 by 5 3/8 by 5 3/8 inches for floor *D*. One piece 11/16 by 5 5/8 by 8 9/16 inches for *E*. Two butts (hinges). One hook and eye.

Lay out and cut sides *A*, as shown in Figure 7*a*. Bore 1 1/8-inch diameter hole through one side. (See fig. 7.) Nail *B*, *C*, and *E* to sides *A*. Hinge floor *D* to *E*. Cover the house with bark. Houses for chickadees and titmice should be placed 6 to 15 feet above the ground. Nuthatch houses should be placed 12 to 20 feet above the ground. Chickadees, titmice, and nuthatches will usually be found in old orchards and along the borders of woodlands.

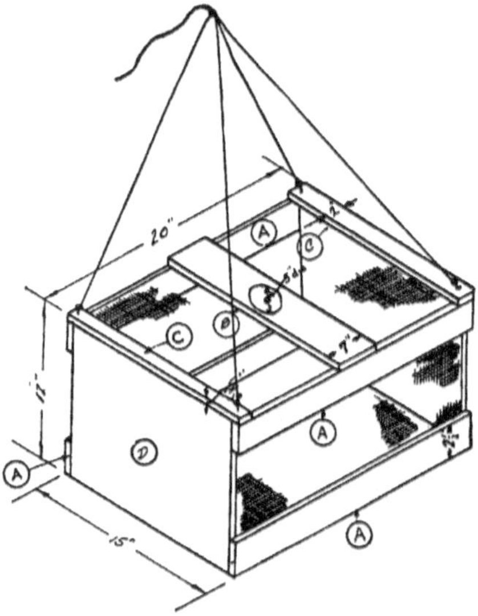

FIGURE 3.—*Live-Bait Box.*—Every boy who fishes knows the value of this simple box.

PART I. OUTDOORS

BLUEBIRD HOUSE

Two pieces 1 1/16 by 6 3/4 by 8 1/2 inches for ends *A*.
Two pieces 1 1/16 by 6 3/4 by 5 inches for sides *B*.
One piece 1 1/16 by 4 1/4 by 8 inches for roof section *C*.
One piece 1 1/16 by 3 9/16 by 8 inches for roof section *D*.
One piece 1 1/16 by 2 1/2 by 10 inches *E*. One piece 1 1/16 by 6 3/4 by 6 3/8 inches for bottom *F*. Two butts (hinges). One hook and eye.

or fence posts, and should be 5 to 10 feet from the ground.

WREN HOUSE

Two pieces 1 1/16 by 5 3/8 by 8 inches for front and back *A*. One piece 1 1/16 by 4 by 5 3/4 inches for sides *B*. One piece 1 1/16 by 5 3/4 by 5 3/8 inches for floor *C*. One piece 1 1/16 by 4 by 6 inches for roof section *D*.

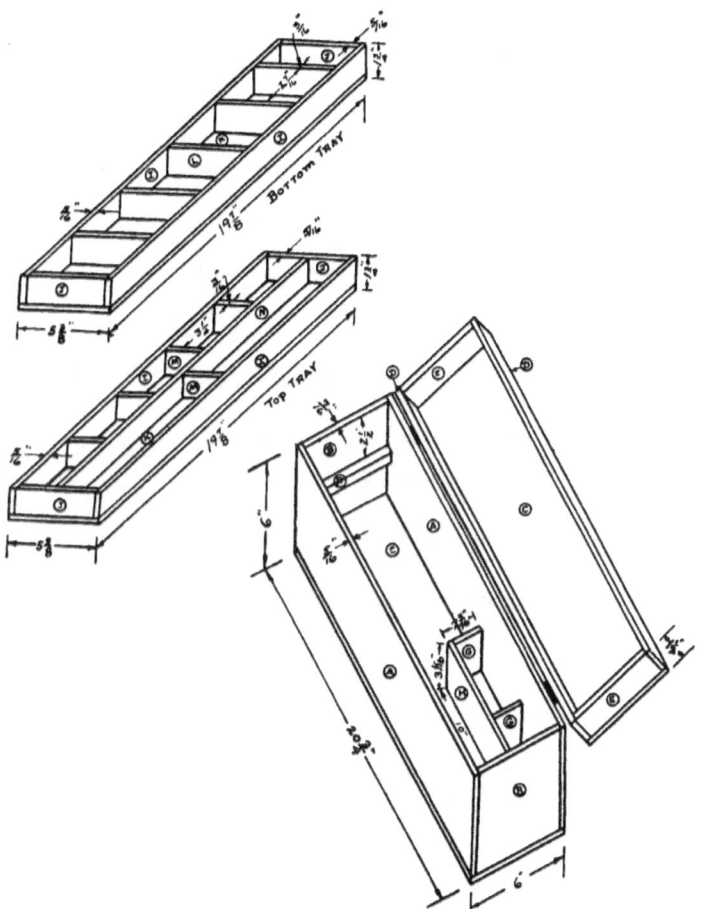

FIGURE 4.—*Fishing-Tackle Box.*—You will be glad that you made this each time you find your tackle in place and well cared for

Shape ends *A* as shown in Figure 8. Bore 1 1/2-inch diameter hole through the front end. Nail ends *A* to sides *B*. Nail roof pieces *C* and *D* to end pieces. The front edges of the roof pieces should project 1 5/8 inches beyond front end *A*. Hinge bottom *F* to rear end of house. Nail *E* to rear end piece *A*. The house may be covered with bark, if desired. Bluebird houses may be fastened to trees

One piece 1 1/16 by 3 5/16 by 6 inches for roof section *E*.
Shape pieces *A* as shown in Figure 9. Cut 1 by 1 1/4-inch opening in front end *A*. Nail front and back pieces *A* to sides *B*. Nail floor *C* to *A* and *B*. Nail roof sections to front and back pieces *A*. Wren houses should be placed 6 to 10 feet above the ground in shady or partly sunlit spaces about the dooryard or in an orchard.

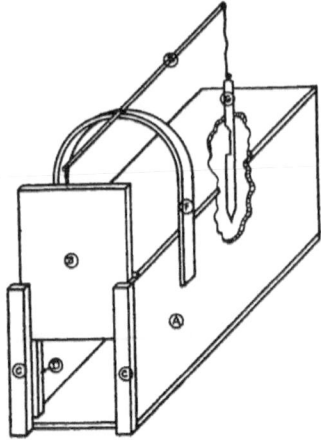

FIGURE 5.—*Rabbit Trap.*—This interesting trap will be worth making

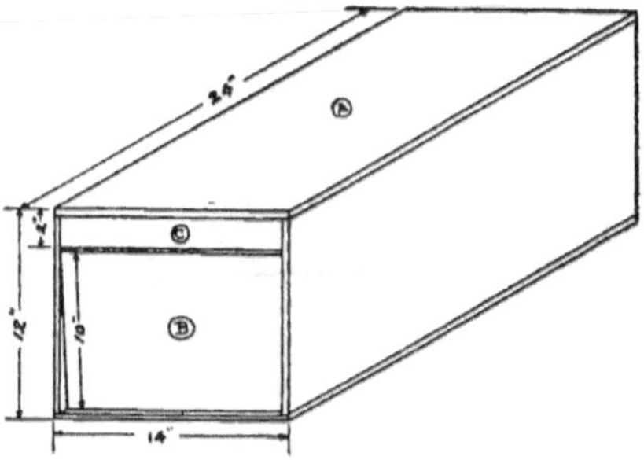

FIGURE 6.—*Water-Turtle Trap.*—Catch a turtle with this trap for your aquarium

FLICKER HOUSE

Two pieces $1\frac{1}{16}$ by $8\frac{3}{8}$ by 18 inches for sides A. One piece $1\frac{1}{16}$ by 7 by 16 inches for front B. One piece $1\frac{1}{16}$ by $8\frac{3}{8}$ by 10 inches for roof C. One piece $1\frac{1}{16}$ by 7 by 18 inches for back D. One piece $1\frac{1}{16}$ by $8\frac{3}{8}$ by $8\frac{3}{8}$ inches for bottom E.

Cut 2½-inch diameter hole through B for entrance. Shape sides A as shown in Figure 10. Bevel top edges of B and D. Nail sides A to B and D; secure bottom E in place. Nail roof C in place. Bark-covered houses are very attractive to flickers and other birds of the woodpecker family. The surfaces of the interior should be unfinished or roughened. One or two inches of coarse sawdust or small chips scattered over the bottom of the box will keep the birds from chipping the house to pieces. Flicker houses should be placed 6 to 20 feet above the ground; that is, above any immediately surrounding foliage.

BARN-OWL HOUSE

Two pieces $1\frac{1}{16}$ by $11\frac{3}{8}$ by 18 inches for ends A. One piece $1\frac{1}{16}$ by $8\frac{1}{2}$ by $21\frac{7}{8}$ inches for roof section B. Two pieces $1\frac{1}{16}$ by $14\frac{3}{4}$ by 18 inches for sides C. One piece $1\frac{1}{16}$ by $7\frac{13}{16}$ by $21\frac{7}{8}$ inches for roof section D. One piece $1\frac{1}{16}$ by $11\frac{3}{8}$ by $19\frac{3}{8}$ inches for floor E.

Shape both ends A as shown in Figure 11. Cut 6-inch diameter hole in front end A. Nail ends A to sides C. Construct roof from pieces B and D as shown. Nail floor E to sides C and ends A. Attach house to trunk of large tree 12 to 18 feet above the ground, or near barn cupolas or little frequented spots about buildings.

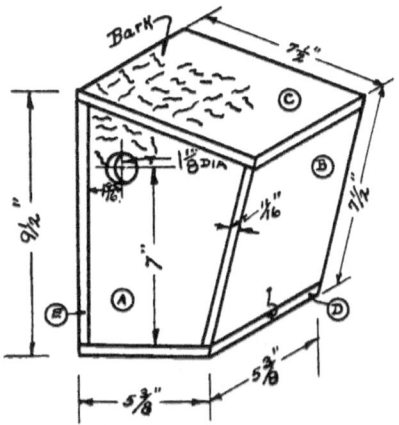

FIGURE 7.—*Chickadee, Titmouse, or Nuthatch House.*—Any titmouse, nuthatch, or chickadee will welcome a house like this

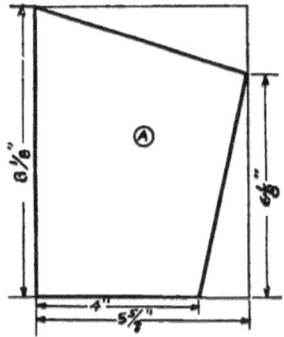

FIGURE 7A.—Detail of sides A

PART I. OUTDOORS

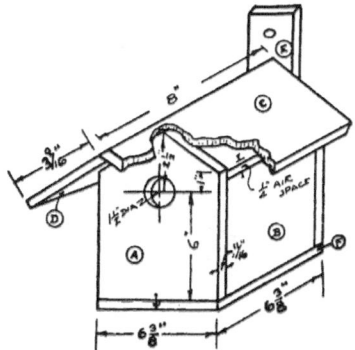

FIGURE 8.—*Bluebird House.*—Make this for bluebirds and hang it where they will use it

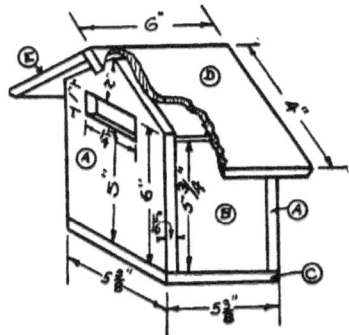

FIGURE 9.—*Wren House.*—Here is an unusually attractive birdhouse for ornamenting the lawn

ROBIN, CATBIRD, OR BROWN THRASHER SHELTER

One piece $\frac{7}{16}$ by $8\frac{7}{16}$ by 16 inches for back A. One piece $\frac{7}{16}$ by 8 by $8\frac{7}{16}$ inches for roof B. One piece $\frac{7}{16}$ by 6 by 8 inches for side C. One piece $\frac{7}{16}$ by 6 by $8\frac{7}{16}$ inches for floor D. One piece $\frac{7}{16}$ by 3 by 3 inches for 2 brackets E.

Round off the top end of A as shown in Figure 12. Shape side C and nail D to C. Secure C and D to A. Cut 3 by 3 inch square piece diagonally across ends to form brackets E. Nail brackets E to A and underside of D. Nail roof B to A and C. These shelters should be placed 6 to 15 feet above the ground in partly shaded spots along the main branches of trees or in the shelter of overhanging eaves of a shed or porch roof.

SWALLOW OR PHŒBE NEST SHELF

One piece $\frac{9}{16}$ by 6 by 8 inches, A. Two pieces $\frac{9}{16}$ by $4\frac{1}{4}$ by 6 inches, B. One piece $\frac{9}{16}$ by $2\frac{1}{2}$ by 8 inches, C. Two pieces $\frac{9}{16}$ by 1 by 4 inches for cleats D.

Bevel pieces marked B so as to fit together as shown in figure 13. Nail cleats D to the underside of B. Nail cleats and pieces marked B to A. Nail C across the ends of B. Place shelf under eaves of buildings, 8 to 12 feet above the ground, preferably near small bodies of water.

SONG-SPARROW SHELTER

Two pieces $\frac{7}{16}$ by 1 by $6\frac{7}{8}$ inches for A. Two pieces $\frac{7}{16}$ by 1 by $6\frac{7}{8}$ inches for B. One piece $\frac{7}{16}$ by $6\frac{7}{8}$ by $6\frac{7}{8}$ inches for floor C. Four pieces $\frac{7}{16}$ by $\frac{3}{4}$ by 5 inches for posts D. Two triangular shaped pieces $\frac{7}{16}$ by $3\frac{1}{2}$ by $3\frac{1}{2}$ by 6 inches for gables E. One piece $\frac{7}{16}$ by $4\frac{1}{16}$ by $8\frac{7}{8}$ inches for roof section F. One piece $\frac{7}{16}$ by $4\frac{1}{2}$ by $8\frac{7}{8}$ inches for roof section G.

Nail pieces A to B; to these nail floor C. Cut roof gables E as shown in Figure 14. Nail posts D (in each of the four corners of the base) to inner side of pieces marked A. Nail gables E to tops of posts D. Cut tops of posts flush with gables. Nail roof pieces F and G to gables E. Place shelter 2 or 3 feet from the ground in thickets, shrubbery, or hedges.

FINCH HOUSE

Two pieces $1\frac{1}{16}$ by 6 by $7\frac{3}{8}$ inches for ends A. Two pieces $1\frac{1}{16}$ by $3\frac{3}{4}$ by 6 inches for sides B. One piece $1\frac{1}{16}$ by 5 by $8\frac{7}{8}$ inches for roof section C. One piece $1\frac{1}{16}$ by $7\frac{3}{8}$ by $7\frac{3}{8}$ inches for floor D. One piece $1\frac{1}{16}$ by $4\frac{9}{16}$ by $8\frac{7}{8}$ inches for roof section E.

Shape ends A as shown in Figure 15. Cut 2-inch diameter hole in the front end. Nail ends A to sides B. To these nail floor D. Roof sections C and E are secured to ends A. Place finch houses 8 to 12 feet above the ground in orchards or dooryards containing shrubbery.

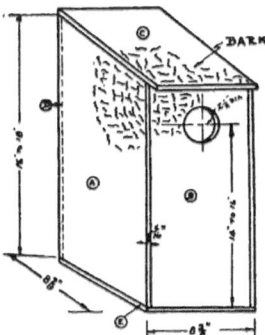

FIGURE 10.—*Flicker House.*—The bark-covered surface of this house will attract flickers

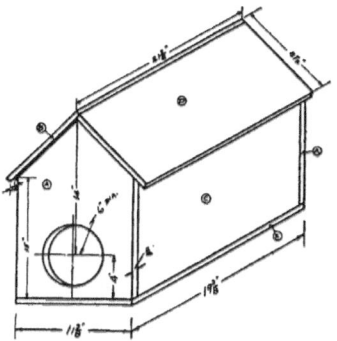

FIGURE 11.—*Barn-Owl House.*—Homes for these birds must be large and this model is just right

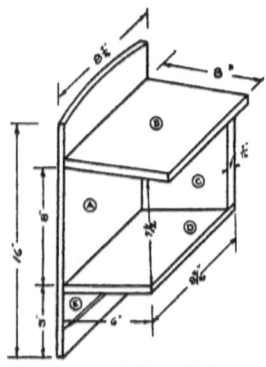

FIGURE 12.—*Robin, Catbird, or Brown Thrasher Shelter.*—Such birds will take advantage of this type of shelter

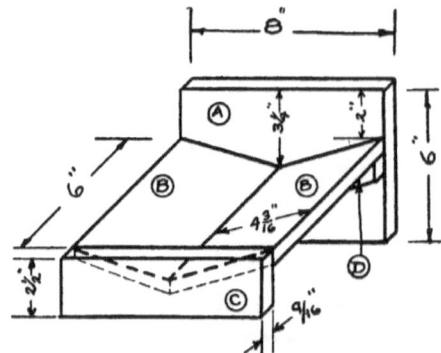

FIGURE 13.—*Swallow or Phoebe Nest Shelf.*—Fasten this under the eaves for the swallows to use

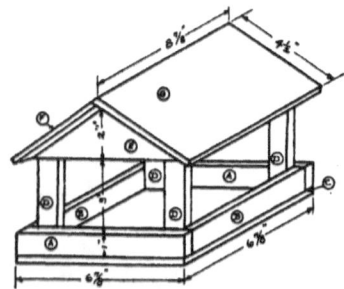

FIGURE 14.—*Song Sparrow Shelter.*—Designed for small birds and quite easily made

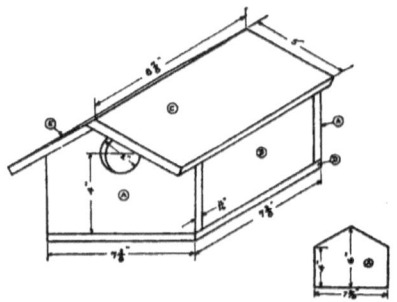

FIGURE 15.—*Finch House.*—Finches are attracted to a house of this kind

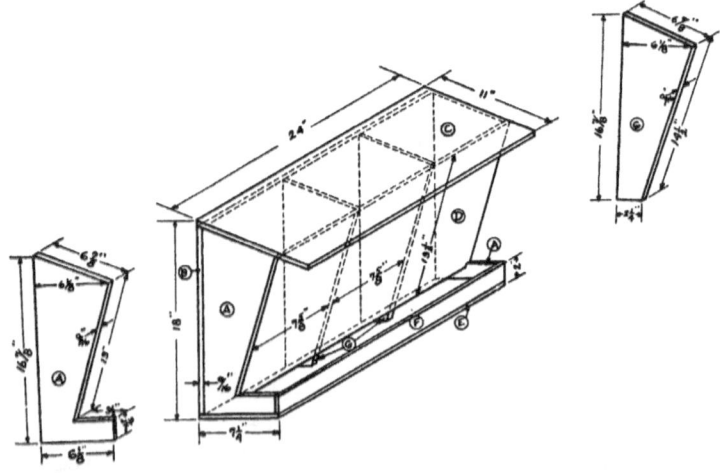

FIGURE 16.—*Bird Feed Box.*—Saves feed and makes less mess

BIRD FEED BOX

Four pieces $\frac{9}{16}$ by $6\frac{1}{8}$ by $16\frac{7}{8}$ inches for ends *A* and partitions *G*. One piece $\frac{9}{16}$ by $16\frac{7}{8}$ by 24 inches for back *B*. One piece $\frac{9}{16}$ by 11 by 24 inches for lid *C*. One piece $\frac{9}{16}$ by $13\frac{1}{2}$ by 24 inches for front *D*. One piece $\frac{9}{16}$ by $7\frac{1}{4}$ by 24 inches for bottom *E*. One piece $\frac{9}{16}$ by $1\frac{7}{16}$ by 24 inches for *F*. One pair butts (hinges).

Shape ends *A* and partitions *G* as shown in Figure 16. Nail back *B*, bottom *E*, and strip *F* to ends *A*. Notch bottom corners of front *D* and nail to ends *A*, as shown. Nail partitions *G* to *B* and *D*. Hinge lid *C* to back *B* with two $1\frac{1}{2}$-inch butts. Crushed bones, bird seed, buckwheat, crumbs, cracked corn, crushed peanuts, and chopped nuts of various kinds—all make excellent bird feed.

BIRD FEEDING HOUSE (REVOLVING)

Two pieces $\frac{7}{16}$ by 4 by $5\frac{1}{4}$ inches for ends *A*. One piece $\frac{7}{16}$ by 4 by 16 inches for floor *B*. One piece $\frac{7}{16}$ by $4\frac{1}{4}$ by 16 inches for roof *C*. One piece $\frac{7}{16}$ by 4 by $15\frac{1}{8}$ inches for back *D*. One piece $\frac{7}{16}$ by 1 by $15\frac{1}{8}$ inches for cleat *E*. Two pieces $\frac{7}{16}$ by 4 by 10 inches for vanes *F*. One dowel $\frac{1}{2}$ inch diameter by $16\frac{7}{8}$ inches for *G*. One metal rod $\frac{1}{4}$ inch diameter for pivot *H*.

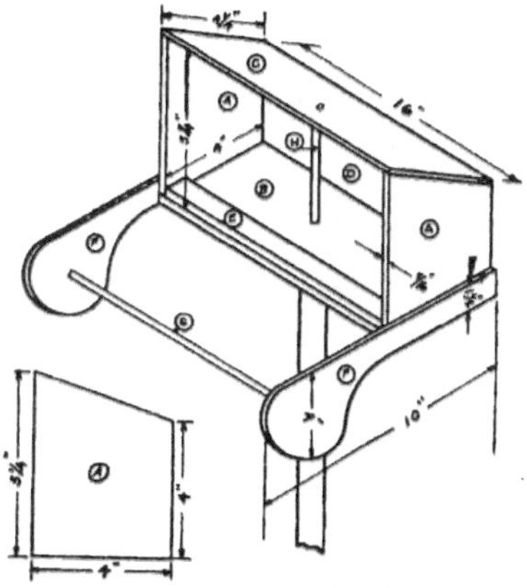

FIGURE 17.—*Bird Feeding House (revolving)*.—This feeder revolves with the wind and thus protects both birds and food

Shape ends *A* as shown in Figure 17. Construct house by nailing *B* and *C* to ends *A*. Ends *A*, floor *B*, and roof *C* are all nailed to back *D*. Nail cleat *E* to floor *B*. Shape vanes *F* as shown, then nail them to ends *A* of house. Dowel *G* is fitted into holes bored through the large ends of the vanes. The house is pivoted on a post, so that it will be free to revolve with the wind.

MAIL BOX

One piece 11 inches high cut from one end of box for door, *A*. One piece $1\frac{1}{16}$ by $7\frac{1}{16}$ by 26 inches for roof section *B*. One box 24 by 11 by $14\frac{1}{2}$ inches, *C*. One piece $1\frac{1}{16}$ by $6\frac{3}{8}$ by 26 inches for roof section *D*. Two butts (hinges). One hinge hasp and lock.

Cut ends and sides of box *C* as shown in Figure 18. Cut one end of box to form door; in this door a 1 by 7 inch opening is cut to allow mail to be placed in box. The angle of this opening should slope sharply upwards, to prevent rain from entering. The door is then hinged to side of box. Nail roof sections *B* and *D* in place. Secure hinge hasp to side of box as shown. A wire paper holder may be fastened to the side of the box for newspapers and magazines.

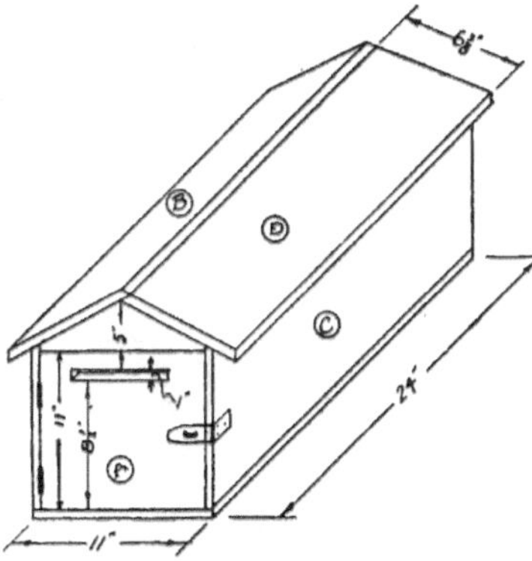

FIGURE 18.—*Mail Box*.—A necessary article for either camp or cottage

ICELESS REFRIGERATOR

Four pieces $\frac{25}{32}$ by $1\frac{3}{4}$ by 42 inches for leg strips *A*. Four pieces $\frac{25}{32}$ by 1 by 42 inches for leg strips *B*. Four pieces $\frac{9}{16}$ by 1 by $14\frac{7}{16}$ inches, *C*. Four pieces $\frac{9}{16}$ by 1 by $11\frac{5}{16}$ inches, *D*. One piece $\frac{5}{16}$ by $12\frac{7}{16}$ by $14\frac{7}{16}$ inches, *E*. Four pieces $\frac{9}{16}$ by $\frac{9}{16}$ by $14\frac{7}{16}$ inches, *F*. Four pieces $\frac{9}{16}$ by $\frac{9}{16}$ by $12\frac{7}{16}$ inches, *G*. Two pieces $\frac{25}{32}$ by $1\frac{3}{4}$ by 37 inches for door strips *H*. Two pieces $\frac{25}{32}$ by $1\frac{3}{4}$ by $12\frac{1}{2}$ inches for door strips *I*. One piece $\frac{25}{32}$ by $1\frac{3}{4}$ by $39\frac{1}{8}$ inches for door diagonal brace *J*. Three brass butts (hinges). Rustless wire screening. Poultry netting. One pan 14 by 16 inches. One pan 17 by 18 inches. Canton flannel, burlap, or duck.

Construct framework by nailing leg strips *A* and *B* and braces *C* and *D* together as shown in Figure 19. As the framework is to be covered with wire screening, this screening should be measured and secured to the inner sides of the leg strips before braces *C* and *D* are nailed to the leg strips. The wire screening should extend over top braces *C* and *D* as shown. Nail bottom *E* to bottom braces *C* and *D*. Pieces *F* and *G* are used to construct the framework of the two shelves; these pieces are joined together by corner lap joints. (See fig. 19.) The shelf frames are covered with poultry netting. Construct door frame by joining pieces *H* and *I* together as shown (corner lap joints are again used). Shape ends of diagonal *J* and nail it to doorframe members *H* as shown. Cover the door with wire screening. Hinge the door to leg strip *A* as shown. The shelves may be supported on small blocks of wood secured to the leg strips. The smaller pan is placed on top of the framework, while the framework stands in the larger pan.

It is suggested that all woodwork, shelves and pans be coated with two coats of white paint, and one or two coats of white enamel.

A cover of canton flannel, burlap, or duck should be made to fit the frame. Put the smooth side out if canton flannel is used. Approximately 3 yards of material will be needed. The cover is to be buttoned around the top of the frame and down the side on which the door is not hinged. Large-head tacks and eyelets worked in the material answer the purpose. On the front side arrange the tacks on the top of the door instead of on the frame, and fasten the cover down the latch side of the door, allowing a wide hem of the material to overlap the place where the door closes. The door may then be opened without unbuttoning the cover. The bottom of the cover should extend down into the lower pan. Four double strips, which taper to 8 or 10 inches in width, should be sewed to the upper part of the cover to extend into the upper pan.

OPERATION

The lowering of the temperature of the inside of the refrigerator depends upon the evaporation of water. The upper pan should be kept filled with water. The water is drawn by capillary attraction through the wicks and saturates the cover.

Sketch outline of bird desired on the wood, and cut the bird out with a coping or jig saw. Bore a ½-inch hole for dowel stick as shown, about 1 inch deep. Insert dowel in hole and drive the other end, which should be sharpened, into the ground. (See fig. 20.) A number of these birds on sticks highly colored, add a great deal to the appearance of the lawn or flower bed.

DOOR KNOCKER

One piece 1¹⁄₁₆ by 3 by 8½ inches for base *A*. Two pieces 1¹⁄₁₆ by 2 by 2½ inches for *B*. One

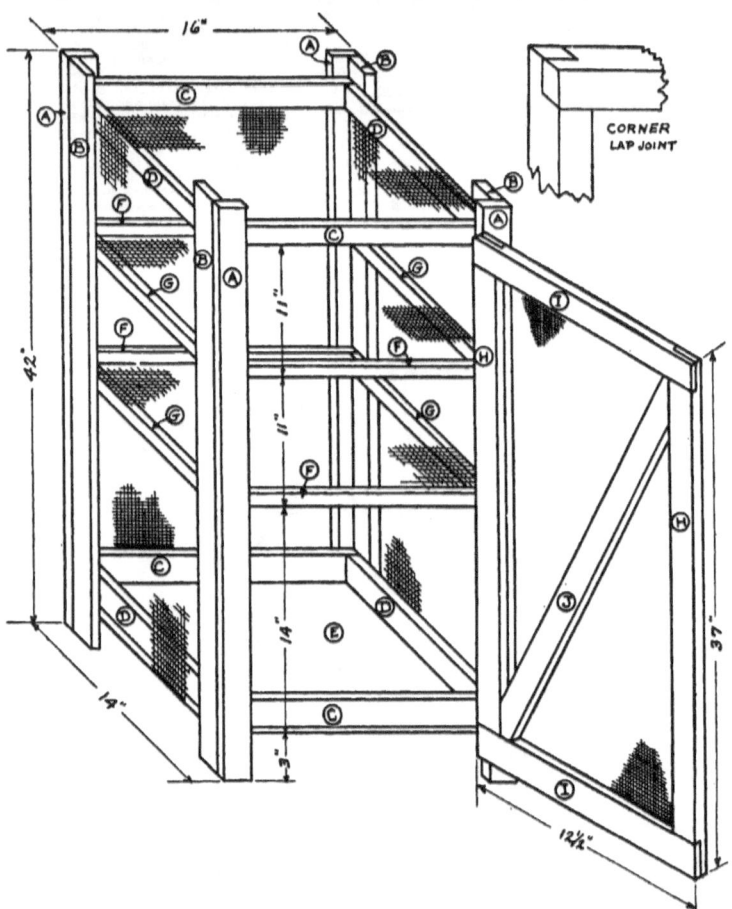

FIGURE 19.—*Iceless Refrigerator.*—The camp cook will be glad to have you provide this clever comfort. Courtesy United States Department of Agriculture

Capillary action starts more readily if the cover is first dampened. Since the temperature in the refrigerator will be lower in proportion to the evaporation of moisture in the cover, the refrigerator should be set in the shade, where wind blows freely.

GARDEN STICK

One piece plywood or other wood ⁹⁄₁₆ by 5 by 6 inches. One piece ½-inch doweling approximately 48 inches long.

curved round stick about 5½ inches long, *C*. One block of knotty wood for hammer *D*.

Shape pieces marked *B* as shown in Figure 21. Nail these pieces securely to base *A*. Suspend handle *C* between pieces marked *B*. Drive a tack in the end of hammer *D* and another in base *A*, so that the heads will come together when the hammer is against the base. A small piece of spring steel against the upper end will cause the hammer to strike the base with considerable force, upon releasing it.

PART I. OUTDOORS

BARREL-STAVE HAMMOCK

Barrel staves or boards, strung with stout rope knotted, may be used for the hammock shown in Figure 22. The knots are on the under side of the staves, or boards; therefore they do not show in the picture. They are necessary to keep the staves from sliding against each other.

FOLDING TABLE TOP

Four boards 1 1/16 by 7 by 48 inches. Six butts (hinges).

You may want a larger or smaller table; if so, the lengths and widths of the boards may be altered to suit your needs. The boards are hinged together

FOLDING TABLE

One piece 7/16 by 10 7/8 by 36 inches, A. Two pieces 7/16 by 10 by 30 inches, B. Two tops 7/16 by 29 9/16 by 36 inches, C. Four pieces 7/16 by 1 1/8 by 30 inches for legs D. Four pieces 7/16 by 1 1/8 by 29 9/16 inches, E. Two pieces 7/16 by 1 1/8 by 31 1/2 inches, F. Two pieces 7 7/16 by 10 by 35 1/8 inches, G. Three pieces 7/16 by 10 by 14 9/16 inches for partitions K. Eight butts (hinges).

Construct the central box framework by nailing pieces A, B, and G together as shown in Figure 25. Edges of A should overlap edges of B 7/16 inch. Nail partitions K in place, two between pieces marked G, and the other between A and G. Construct table tops C by cleating boards together with cleats

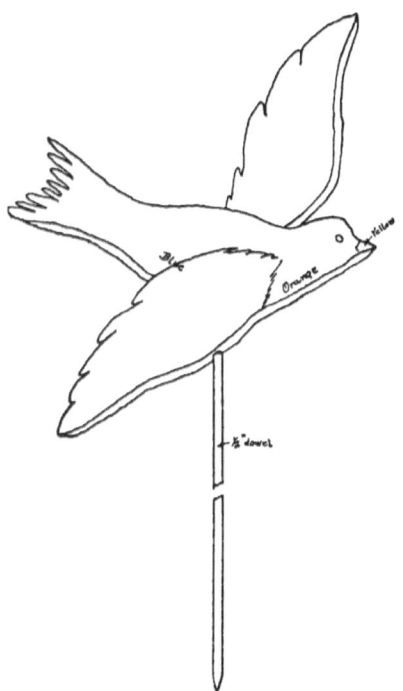

FIGURE 20.—*Garden Stick.*—A vivid bit of color in bird form, is attractive when stuck in among the plants

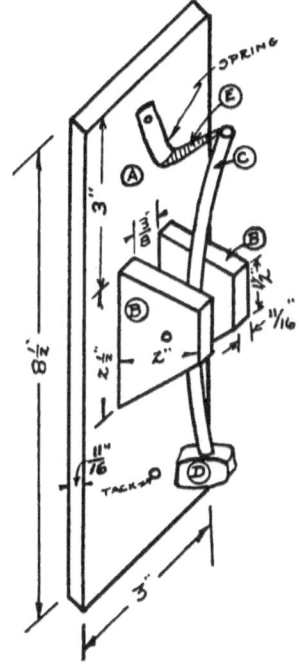

FIGURE 21.—*Door Knocker.*—This is an ingenious little device and is fun to make.

as shown in Figure 23. Notice that the two center hinges are placed on one side of the top, while the other four are placed on the other side. The top may then be folded up so the boards lie on top of each other.

TABLE HORSE

One piece 25/32 by 2 1/2 by 31 1/8 inches, A. Four pieces 25/32 by 2 1/2 by 32 inches, B. Two pieces 9/16 by 2 1/2 by 13 11/16 inches, C. One piece 9/16 by 2 1/2 by 28 7/16 inches, D. Eight pieces 9/16 by 9/16 by 2 1/2 inches for blocks, F.

Shape ends of legs B as shown in Figure 24, and nail pieces C and E to legs B. Nail brace D to pieces marked C. Nail blocks F to ends of A and slip A in place, as shown.

109033°—30——3

E as shown. Hinge legs D to tops C. Nail strips F to C between legs D. Hinge tops C to A. The legs may then be folded up flat against the underside of tops C, which in turn fold down flat against B and G.

WEATHER VANE

One 9/16-inch board—length and width will depend on size of fish desired. One piece steel rod 3/16-inch diameter about 24 inches in length. Two pieces stiff wire.

Either sketch the fish or trace the outline of a picture of one on the board. Cut the fish out with a coping saw. Bore a 3/16-inch hole in the bottom edge of the fish at a point about 1 inch toward the head from the center, to a depth of about three-fourths

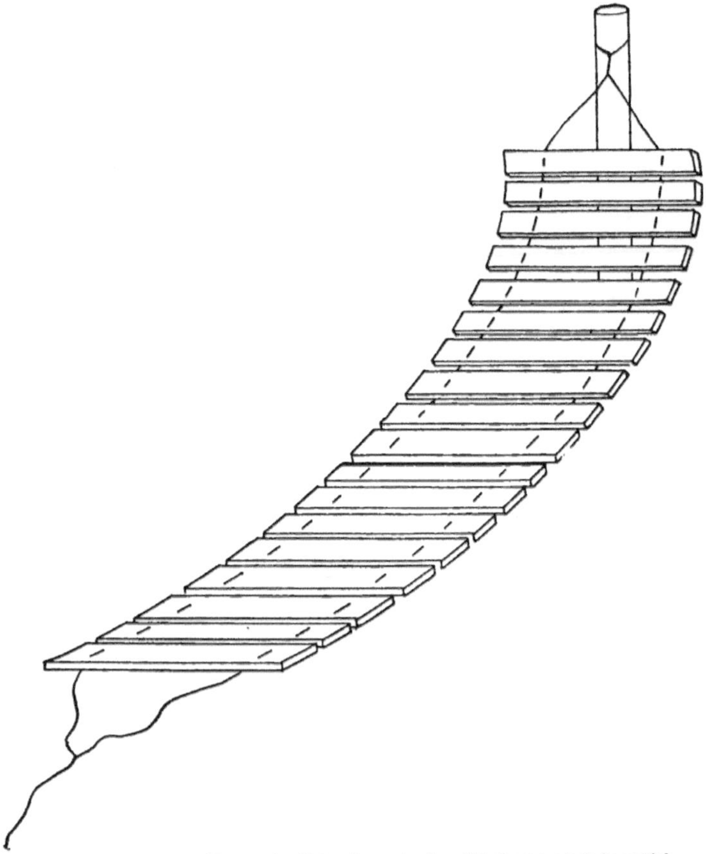

FIGURE 22.—*Barrel-Stave Hammock.*—Not quite so simple as it looks if made to be restful

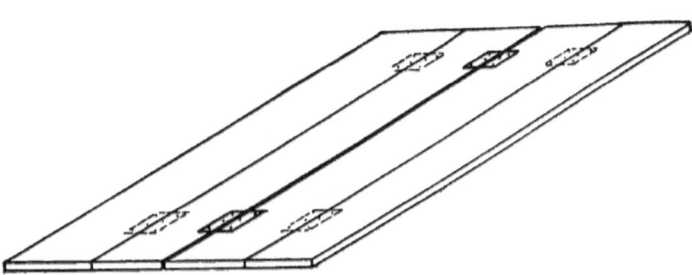

FIGURE 23.—*Folding Table Top.*—A convenient table top which folds up when not in use

PART I. OUTDOORS 13

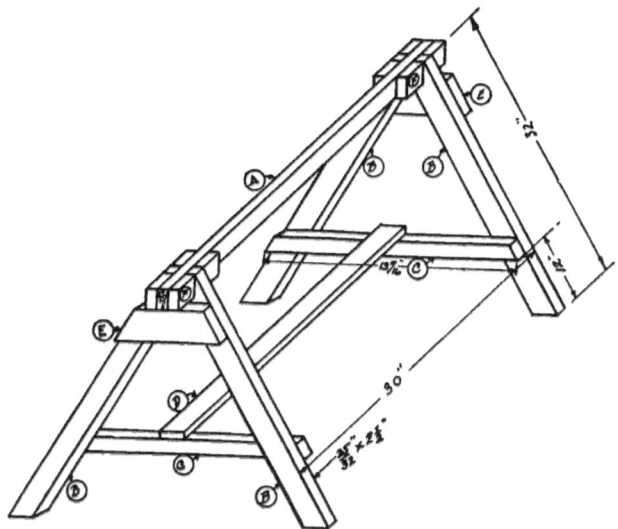

FIGURE 24.—*Table Horse.*—You will be able to construct this useful article with a small amount of trouble

the width of the fish. (See fig. 26.) The hole should be reamed out so the rod will fit loosely in the hole. Letters may be cut from wood or shaped from wire and secured to stiff wires which in turn should be soldered to the steel rod.

SHOWER

One tight barrel (one that will hold water). One short piece of pipe threaded at both ends. One sprinkler.
Bore a hole slightly smaller in diameter than that of the piece of pipe, in one head of the barrel. Attach the sprinkler to the pipe and screw the other end of the pipe into the hole bored in the head of the barrel. (See fig. 27.) A trapdoor should be cut and fitted into the top head of the barrel, in order to fill it with water. The barrel must, of course, be supported on some sort of trestle arrangement.

HURDLE

Two pieces ⅝ by 1½ by 30 inches, *A*. Two pieces ⅝ by 1½ by 24 inches, *B*. Six pieces 1¼ by 1½ by 23 inches for legs *C* and braces *D*. Two blocks 1¼ by 1½ by 1½ inches, *E*. One piece 1¼ by 1½ by 32¹³⁄₁₆ inches, *F*. One bolt 34½ inches in length, *G*.

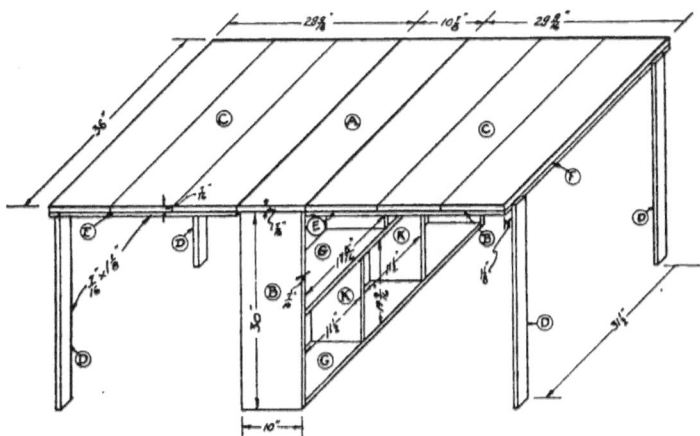

FIGURE 25.—*Folding Table.*—Several of these tables may be needed. They are much less expensive to make than to buy

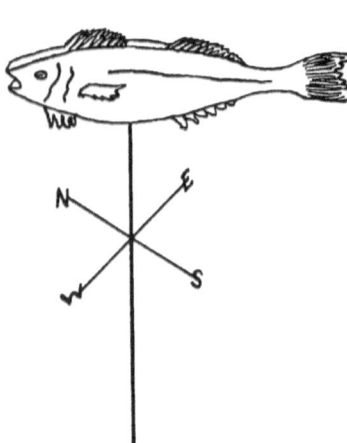

FIGURE 26.—*Weather Vane.*—To know "which way the wind blows" it is advisable to have a weather vane

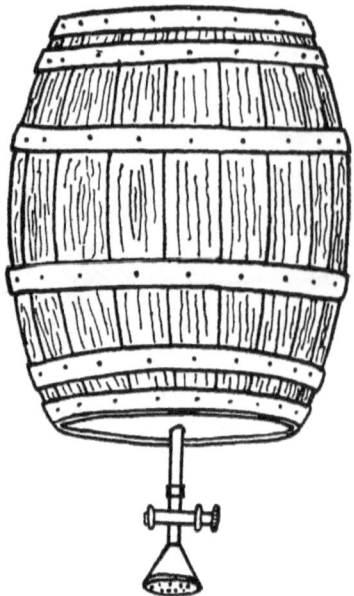

FIGURE 27.—*Shower.*—If you miss the home tub, try this shower

Nail pieces A and B together as shown in Figure 28. Construct triangular shaped supports by nailing pieces C, D, and E together as shown. Note that blocks E are placed between triangle legs C. Bore a hole through peak of supports for bolt to pass through. Secure triangular-shaped ends in an upright position as shown by nailing F to bottom brace D and putting bolt G in place. The hurdle framework is then secured to bolt G by strap hinges or piece of metal bent as shown.

STILE

Three pieces 25/32 by 2½ by 35 inches, A. Two pieces 25/32 by 2½ inches, of sufficient length to extend 18 inches above the top wire of the fence, for B. Two pieces 25/32 by 2½ inches for braces C.

Nail cross pieces A, each directly above each wire, to the post as shown in Figure 29. Nail upright pieces B to ends of A. Cut and nail braces C to post and bottom ends of uprights B.

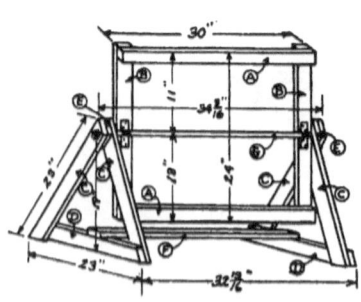

FIGURE 28.—*Hurdle.*—This hurdle, which revolves, will not fall if touched by the runner

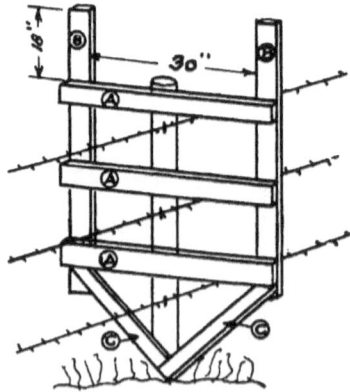

FIGURE 29.—*Stile.*—Save your clothes and the wire fence by using this stile

PART I. OUTDOORS

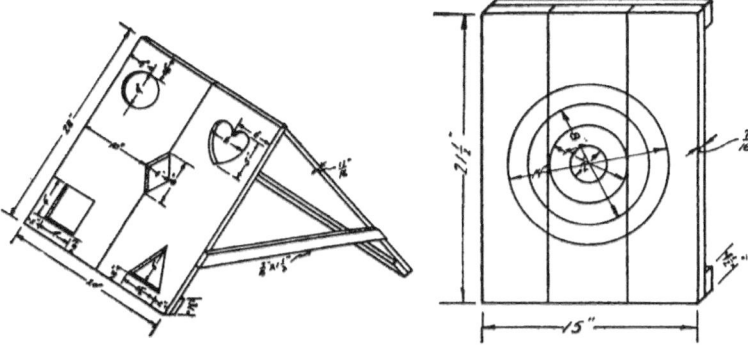

FIGURE 30.—*Bean-Bag Target.*—A good bean bag target

FIGURE 31.—*Dart Target.*—This little target will help you develop a good aim

BEAN-BAG TARGET

Two boards 13/16 by 24 by 28 inches. Two pieces 7/16 by 1½ by 12 inches for braces.
If the boards are made up of several pieces, cleats 5/16 by 1 inch may be used to hold them together. The boards may be hinged or nailed together as shown in Figure 30. If the boards are hinged together, a piece of chain or rope may be used to keep them at the correct distance apart; otherwise, two cleats nailed to the edges of the boards should be used. It will be necessary to use your keyhole saw to cut out the varied shaped holes in the boards.

DART TARGET

Two or three 7/16-inch boards, 21½ inches in length, of sufficient width to make one piece 15 by 21½ inches. Two pieces 7/16 by 1½ by 15 inches for cleats.
If the target is constructed of several pieces, they should be cleated together as shown in Figure 31. Lay out the 2, 4, 8, and 14 inch circles. The target may be suspended by a screw eye, screwed in the top cleat.

AUTO JACK

One piece 13/16 by 5¼ by 22 inches, A. One bolt ⅜ by 6 inches.
Cut a piece out of the center of A 2½ by 19 inches. (See fig. 32.) From the piece removed cut a piece 14 inches in length. Cut a notch in one end. Bore a ½-inch hole 1 inch from the other end through the center of the piece removed. Bore ½-inch holes through the bottom ends of A for the ⅜-inch bolt

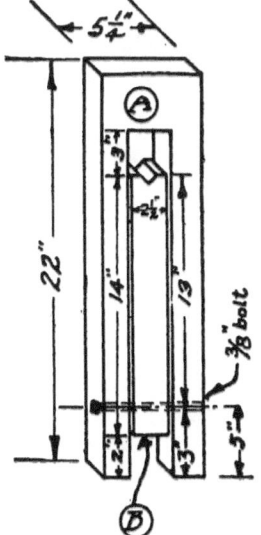

FIGURE 32.—*Auto Jack.*—Can be used for more than one purpose in the camp. Courtesy Michigan Agricultural College

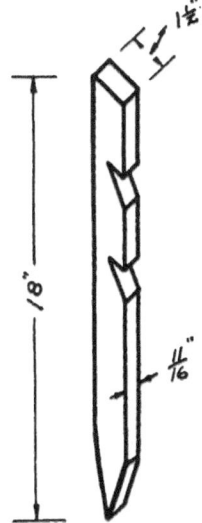

FIGURE 33.—*Tent Peg.*—These are absolutely necessary for the tent camp, and any boy can make them

FIGURE 34.—*Beach Sandal.*—A great convenience at the beach

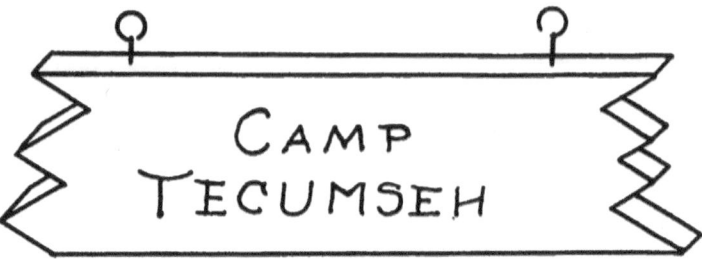

FIGURE 35.—*Sign.*—Vote for a popular camp name and put it on a signboard like this to identify your camp

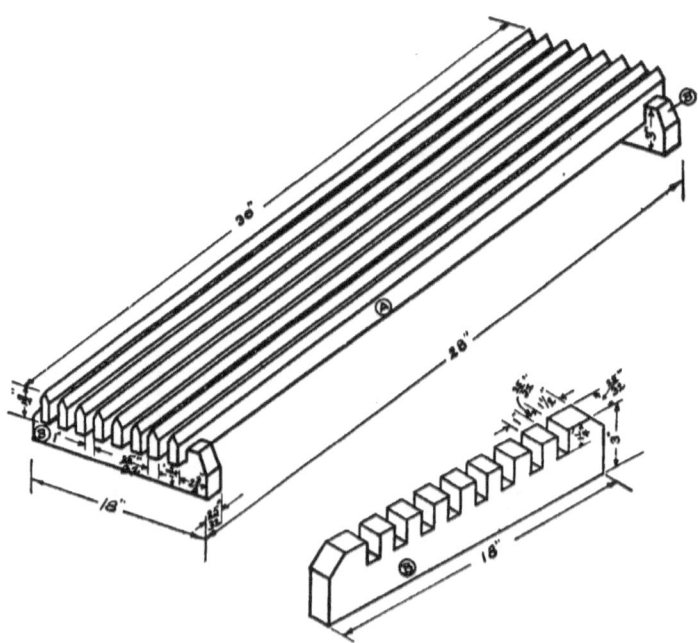

FIGURE 36.—*Foot Scraper.*—Especially useful on a muddy day

PART I. OUTDOORS

as shown. A cleat nailed across the top of *A* will keep it from splitting.

To operate the jack, place *A* flat on the ground and *B* in a vertical position with the notch under the hub cap. Then pull *A* up to a vertical position.

TENT PEG

One piece 1 1/16 by 1 1/2 by 18 inches.

Cut notches 4 inches from the top end, about 4 inches apart. Sharpen lower end of peg as shown in Figure 33.

BEACH SANDAL

One piece 7/8 by 4 by 12 inches.

Sketch the outline of your foot on the board. Cut out the sandal. Straps, nailed to the sandal in such a manner as to pass over the instep and toes, serve to keep the sandal on the foot. (See fig. 34.)

SIGN

One board any size, about 1 1/16 inch in thickness. Two wire screw hooks.

Cut the ends of the board as shown in Figure 35. Wire screw hooks are used to support the sign.

inch of each brad protruding; file the protruding ends down to a sharp point. Piece *G* should be nailed to pieces marked *F*, which are in turn nailed to pieces marked *E*; this framework is to be bolted to *A* as shown.

After placing the log to be sawed upon the sawbuck, the framework composed of pieces *E*, *F*, and *G* is rested on the log. While sawing the log, one foot is placed on *G*; the protruding sharp ends of the nails keep the log from turning.

SPRING REFRIGERATOR

One box 30 by 18 by 12 inches, *A*. One piece 1 1/16 inch by inside depth by inside width of box for partition *B*. One galvanized iron box *D* inside width of box *A* by 6 inches by inside depth of box *A*. One hinge hasp. Two butts (hinges).

Bore hole through center of back of box *A* about 2 inches from the top edge; the diameter of this hole should be slightly greater than the outside diameter of the pipe through which the spring water enters the refrigerator. Similar holes are bored through partition *B* and one end of box *A* to allow outflow of water. (See fig. 38.) *B* is then secured inside box *A*. The galvanized iron box is placed in the opposite end of the box. The water in the center

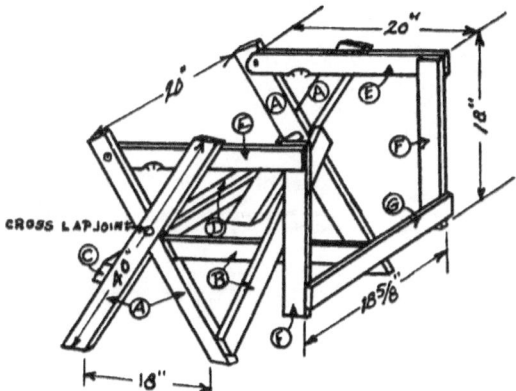

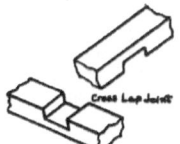

FIGURE 37.—*Sawbuck*.—Logs sawed in this buck can not slip

FIGURE 37A.—Cross lap joint detail

FOOT SCRAPER

Eight pieces 25/32 by 1 3/4 by 30 inches for scrapers *A*. Two pieces 25/32 by 3 by 18 inches for supports *B*. Shape strips *A* and supports *B* as shown in Figure 36. Drive strips *A* into notches in supports *B*; these notches should be so cut as to form a tight fit. Glue should be used to hold strips *A* securely in place.

SAWBUCK

Four pieces 1 5/8 by 3 by 40 inches for legs *A*. Two pieces 1 1/16 by 1 1/2 by 31 inches for cross braces *B*. One piece 1 1/16 by 1 1/2 by 23 1/4 inches for brace *C*. One piece 2-inch diameter round 31 inches in length, *D*. Two pieces 1 1/16 by 1 1/2 by 20 inches, *E*. Two pieces 1 1/16 by 1 1/2 by 18 inches, *F*. One piece 1 1/16 by 1 1/2 by 18 5/8 inches, *G*.

Cut out and nail legs *A* together with cross lap joints as shown in Figure 37. Through the center of each joint bore a 1 3/4-inch diameter hole. Shape both ends of round *D* so as to fit tightly in holes through the cross lap joints. Glue round *D* in place. Nail cross braces *B* and brace *C* to legs *A* as shown. Round one edge of pieces marked *E*. Drive three brads in each round as shown, leaving about 1/2

compartment may be used for drinking purposes. Milk and other bottled and canned foods and drinks may be stored in the partitioned end, standing in the water, while butter, meat, and other foods that should be kept dry, are stored in the galvanized iron box. Hinge lid to box.

SALT BOX (ANIMALS)

One box, any size, about 6 inches deep, *A*. Four cleats 7/16 by 1 1/2 by 6 inches plus length of side of box *B*.

Nail cleats *B* to the sides of box *A* as shown in Figure 39. The projecting ends of the cleats prevent the box from overturning.

CLOTHESLINE REEL

One piece 1 1/16 by 6 by 12 inches. Two pieces 7/16-inch doweling, 5 1/4 inches long.

Bore 7/16-inch holes in the edges of the reel to a depth of 1 inch, as shown in Figure 40. Shape ends as shown. Glue dowels in the holes in the edges. A notch cut in one of the curved ends will be found to be helpful in holding the end of the clothesline, while winding it on the reel.

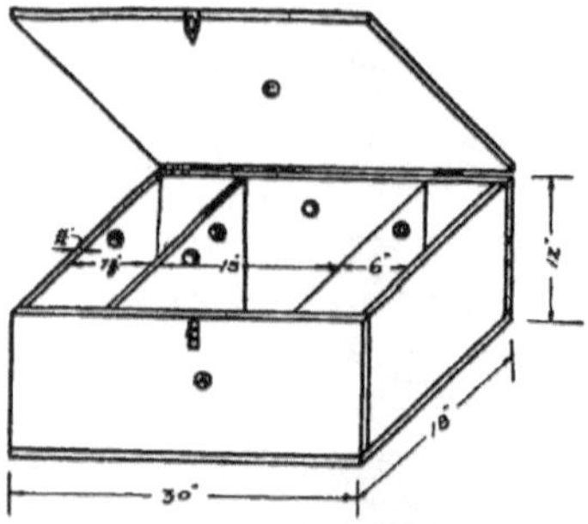

FIGURE 38.—*Spring Refrigerator.*—This refrigerator may be set in the camp spring and its contents thus kept cool

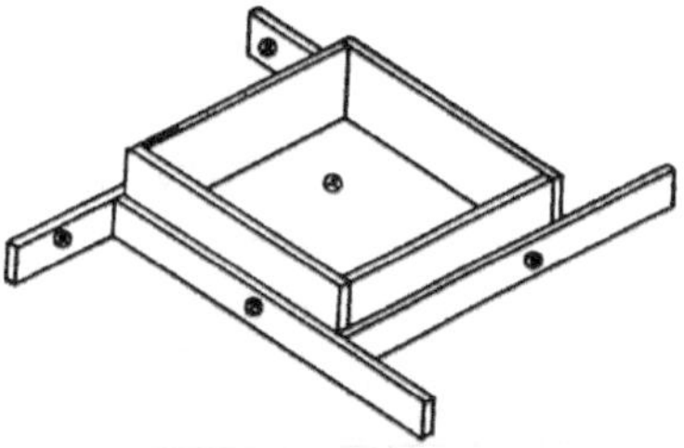

FIGURE 39.—*Salt box (animal's).*—The greatest advantage of this neat salt box is that it can not be overturned

LIGHTHOUSE

One block of wood $1\frac{1}{4}$ by $2\frac{3}{8}$ by $2\frac{3}{8}$ inches for base *A*. One piece $1\frac{3}{8}$-inch round $5\frac{1}{2}$ inches in length *B*.

Shape round *B* as shown in Figure 41; it should be $5\frac{3}{8}$ inches long, $1\frac{3}{8}$ inches diameter at one end, and $\frac{3}{4}$ inch diameter at the other end. Before shaping *B* cut off a piece $\frac{1}{8}$ inch in thickness for collar *C*. Bore a hole through collar *C* of sufficient diameter so that it may be placed on *B* as shown. Top *D* may be whittled out of another piece of wood. Slip collar *C* over the small end of *B* and nail *A* and *D* to *B*. Windows and doors may be painted on *B*.

ORE BOAT

One block $1\frac{5}{16}$ by $2\frac{1}{8}$ by $13\frac{3}{4}$ inches, *A*. One piece $\frac{9}{16}$ by $1\frac{3}{8}$ by 2 inches, *B*. One piece $\frac{5}{8}$-inch dowel $1\frac{3}{4}$ inches long for smokestack *C*. One piece $\frac{9}{16}$ by $1\frac{3}{8}$ by $1\frac{3}{8}$ inches, *D*. One piece $1\frac{1}{16}$ by $\frac{3}{4}$ by 1 inch, *E*. One piece $\frac{3}{16}$ by 1 by $1\frac{1}{8}$ inches, *F*. Two pieces $\frac{3}{8}$-inch dowel 1 inch in length.

Shape block *A* as shown in Figure 42. Bore $\frac{5}{8}$-inch diameter hole $\frac{3}{4}$ inch deep in *B* for smokestack *C*. Secure *B* to *A* with nails or waterproof glue. Secure *F* to *E*, *E* to *D*, and *D* to *A*. Bore $\frac{3}{8}$-inch diameter holes in each end of *A* for dowel pieces *G*.

CANAL BOAT

Two pieces $\frac{5}{16}$ by $1\frac{1}{8}$ by $9\frac{1}{2}$ inches for roof *A*. One block 1 by $1\frac{3}{8}$ by 9 inches for *B*. One block $1\frac{1}{2}$ by $2\frac{3}{8}$ by 14 inches for *C*. Four pieces of $\frac{1}{2}$-inch dowel $1\frac{1}{4}$ inches long.

Shape block *B* as shown in Figure 43. Bevel one edge of each of the two roof sections *A* and secure them to the sloping top of *B*. Bore four $\frac{1}{2}$-inch holes $\frac{5}{8}$ inch deep in the top side of *C* as shown. Insert and glue dowel pieces in these holes.

STEAMBOAT

One piece $1\frac{1}{16}$ by $2\frac{1}{8}$ by 12 inches, *A*. One piece $\frac{5}{8}$ by $1\frac{1}{2}$ by $7\frac{1}{2}$ inches, *B*. One piece $\frac{5}{8}$ by $\frac{7}{8}$ by $1\frac{1}{8}$ inches, *C*. One piece $\frac{3}{16}$ by $1\frac{1}{8}$ by $1\frac{1}{8}$ inches, *D*. Two $\frac{5}{8}$-inch dowels $1\frac{7}{8}$ inches in length for smokestacks *E*. Two $\frac{3}{8}$-inch dowels $\frac{3}{4}$ inch in length, *F*.

Shape block *A* as shown in Figure 44. Nail *B* to *A*, *C* to *B*, and *D* to *C* as shown. Bore two $\frac{5}{8}$-inch holes in *B* for dowels *E*; glue the dowels in the holes. Bore two $\frac{3}{8}$-inch holes in *A* for dowels *F*; these dowels also should be glued in place. Windows and doors may be sketched or painted on pieces marked *B* and *C*.

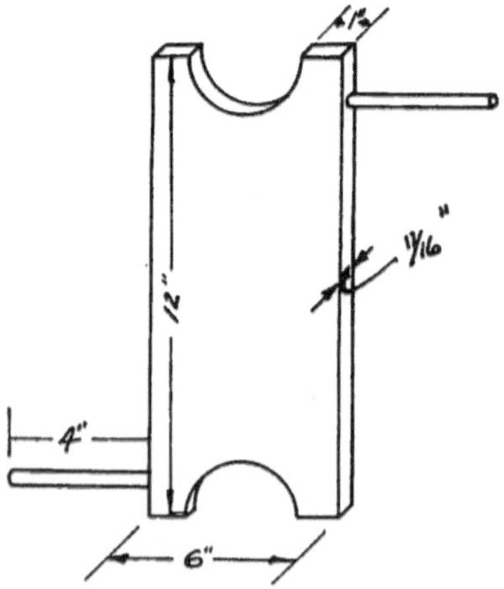

FIGURE 40.—*Clothesline Reel.*—A fine thing to keep the clothesline clean and in good order

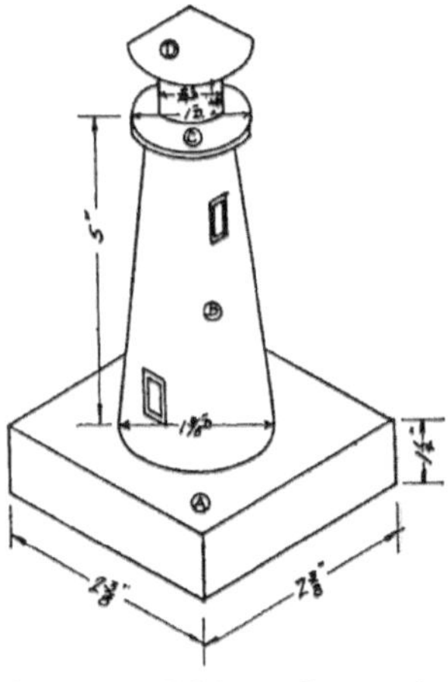

FIGURE 41.—*Lighthouse.*—For your play pool

PART I. OUTDOORS

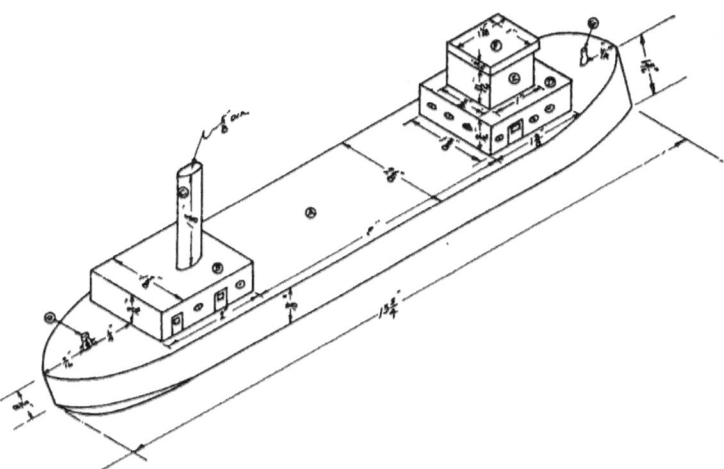

FIGURE 42.—*Ore boat.*—An interesting toy for your little brother

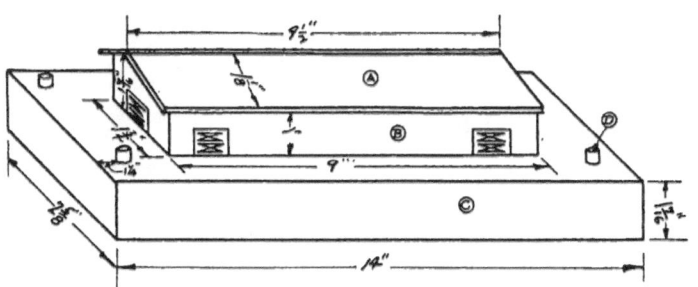

FIGURE 43.—*Canal Boat.*—Be careful to show all the minor points in finishing this boat

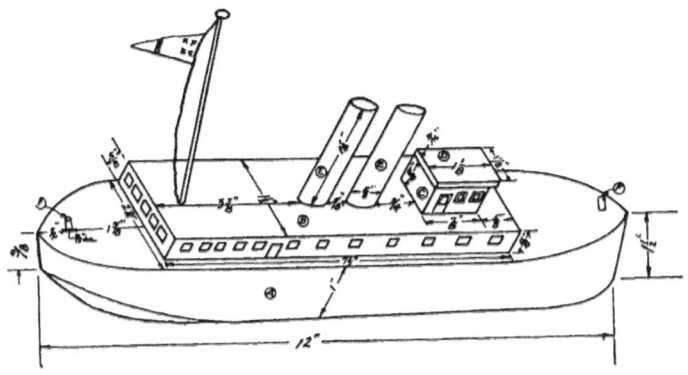

FIGURE 44.—*Steamboat.*—Care must be taken in making this boat

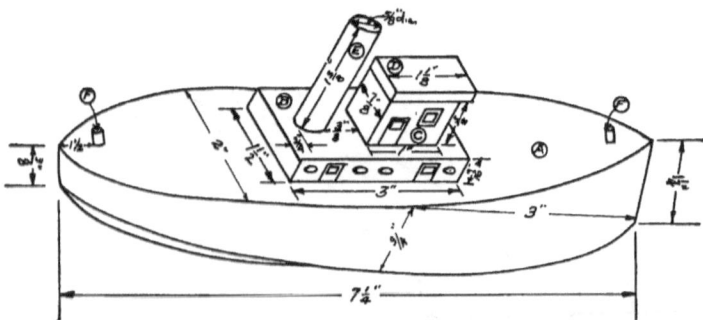

FIGURE 45.—*Tugboat.*—And this one must be made to pull all the others

TUGBOAT

One piece 1¼ by 2 by 7¼ inches, *A*. One piece ⁹⁄₁₆ by 1½ by 3 inches, *B*. One piece 1¹⁄₁₆ by ⅞ by 1 inch, *C*. One piece ⅜ by ⅞ by 1⅛ inches, *D*. One piece ⅜-inch dowel 2 inches long, *E*. Two pieces ¼-inch dowel ½ inch long, *F*.

Shape *A* as shown in Figure 45. Nail *B* to the center of *A*. Nail *C* to *B*, and *D* to *C*. Bore ⅜-inch hole through *B*. Insert dowel *E* in the hole through *B*. Bore holes in *A* for ¼-inch dowels *F*, drive them in place. Windows and doors may be painted on *B* and *C* as shown.

SCOW

One block 1⅜ by 2¾ by 6⅞ inches, *A*. Two pieces of ½-inch dowel, 1 inch long, *B*.

Shape block *A* as shown in Figure 46. Bore two ½-inch dowel holes about ½ inch deep. Force pieces of dowel *B* in these holes as shown.

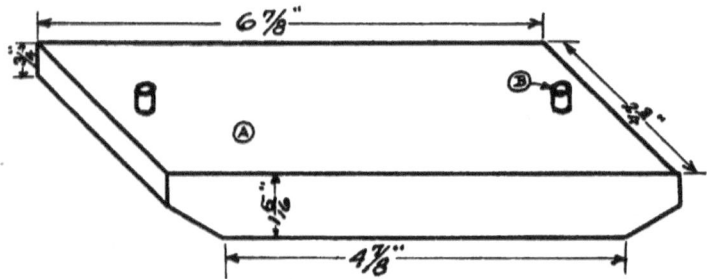

FIGURE 46.—*Scow.*—Wherever you sail your boats this scow would find a place

Part II. INDOORS

FOLDING DRESSING TABLE

Two pieces 7/16 by 12 by 16¼ inches for *A*. Two pieces 9/16 by 5¾ by 12 inches for *B*. Two pieces 7/16 by 5⅝ by 10¾ inches for drawer sides *C*. Two pieces 7/16 by 5⅝ by 15 inches for front and back *D* of drawer. One piece 5/16 by 10¾ by 14⅛ inches for drawer bottom. One piece 7/16 by 5¾ by 15⅛ inches for rear end of box. One mirror 16¼ by 22 inches. Two butts (hinges). Chains.

Construct box by nailing sides *B*, rear end of box, and top and bottom pieces *A* together as shown in Figure 47. Construct drawer by nailing pieces marked *C* and *D* to drawer bottom. Hinge mirror to box as shown. The mirror is secured to the tent pole or wall of the cabin, and the box supported in a horizontal plane by the chains.

ROCKER

One piece 7/16 by 8 by 18 inches for back rest *A*. Two pieces 7/16 by 1⅛ by 36 inches for back supports *B*. One box 18 by 18 by 16 inches for seat *C*. One piece 7/16 by 1½ by 18 inches for crosspieces *D*. Two barrel staves for rockers *E*.

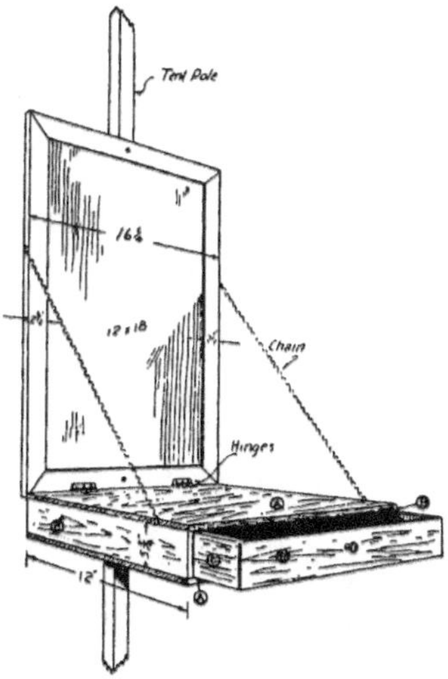

FIGURE 47.—*Folding Dressing Table.*—A convenient dresser for camp use

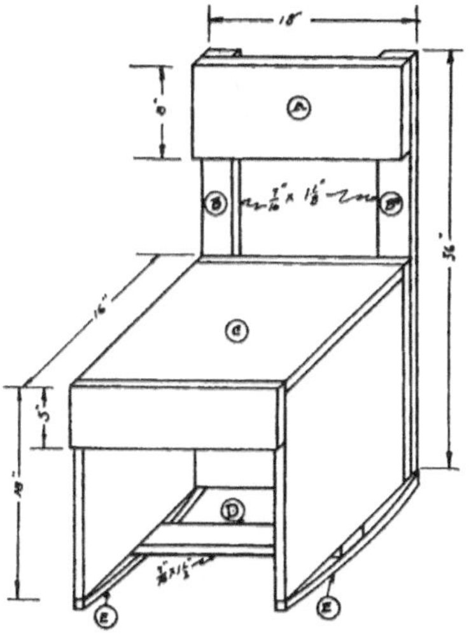

FIGURE 48.—*Rocker.*—A box rocker should go well with the box chair described in this booklet

Remove all of one side of the box with the exception of a piece 5 inches wide, as shown in Figure 48. Nail back *A* to back supports *B*. Supports *B* are then secured to the back of the box as shown. Nail *D* to box, and then secure the barrel staves to box *C* and cross piece *D* as shown.

VANITY

Two boxes 32 by 18 by 13 inches, *A*. One piece 9/16 by 12 by 24 inches, *B*. One piece 9/16 by 12 by 20 inches, *C*. Two boxes inside width by inside depth of *A* by 5⅞ inches for drawers *D*. Two pieces 9/16 by 13 by 30 inches for doors *E*. Four pieces 9/16 by 2 by 14⅛ inches, *F*. Four pieces 9/16 by 2 by 18 inches, *G*. Two pieces 9/16 inch by inside width by inside depth of box *A* for shelves *H*. Eight pieces 11/16 by 1 inch by inside width of box *A* for cleats *I*. One box inside width by inside depth of box *A* by 9 inches, *J*. One box inside width by inside depth of box *A* by 12 inches, *K*. One piece 9/16 by 2½ by 20 inches for brace *L*. One piece 9/16 by 3½ by 3½ inches for brackets *M*. Two pieces 9/16 by 9/16 inches by inside depth of box *A* for cleats N. Four butts (hinges).

Remove one side and one end from boxes marked *A*, and renail lids in place. Nail cleats *N* to shelves *H* and nail shelves *H* in one box *A* at an angle of 60° with the vertical, as shown in Figure 49. Nail drawer cleats *I* to tops and bottoms of boxes *A* as shown. Then nail strips *F* and *G* to open ends of boxes *A*. Next space boxes *A* 20 inches apart and nail rear brace *B* to rear sides of the boxes. Secure brace *L* to inside strips *G*. Nail shelf *C* to *B* and boxes *A*. Brackets *M*, cut from 3½ by 3½ inch square piece, should then be secured in place as shown to help support shelf *C*. Hinge doors *E* to boxes *A* as shown. Hooks and eyes or some other type of fastener may be used to keep doors shut. A mirror may be attached to the vanity or suspended directly over it.

VANITY BENCH

One piece 25/32 by 14 by 30 inches for top *A*. One box 18 by 13 by 9½ inches for legs *B*. Two pieces 9/16 by 1½ by 17½ inches for braces *C*. Two pieces 9/16 by 13 by 18¾ inches, *D*. Four pieces 11/16 by 1½ by 1½ inches for cleats *E*.

Cut box as shown by dotted lines in Figure 50a. Cut a 5 by 6 inch opening in each of legs *B* as shown in Figure 50. Nail pieces *D* to legs *B*. Nail cleats *E* to *D*. Arrange boxes as shown and nail top *A* over the wide ends of *B*. Nail braces *C* to cleats *E*.

The pockets which form the legs provide excellent space for soiled clothes. If desired, a door may be secured in the openings in legs *B* by reversible butts (hinges).

BOOTERY

Two pieces 25/32 by 12 by 20½ inches for ends *A*. One piece 9/16 by 16 by 31¾ inches for back *B*. One piece 9/16 by 3 by 31¾ inches, *C*. One piece 9/16 by 6 9/16 by 22 11/16 inches, *D*. One piece 9/16 by 6 9/16 by 30 9/16 inches, *E*. One piece 9/16 by 6 9/16 by 8⅛ inches, *F*. Two pieces 9/16 by 13 by 15⅞ inches for doors *G*. Two pieces 5/16 by 13 by 30 9/16 inches for shelves *H*. Two pieces 5/16 by 5/16 by 30 9/16 inches for shoe cleats *I*. Two pieces 5/16 by 5/16 by 12 inches for cleat *K*. Five pieces 3/16 by 2 11/16 by 12 inches

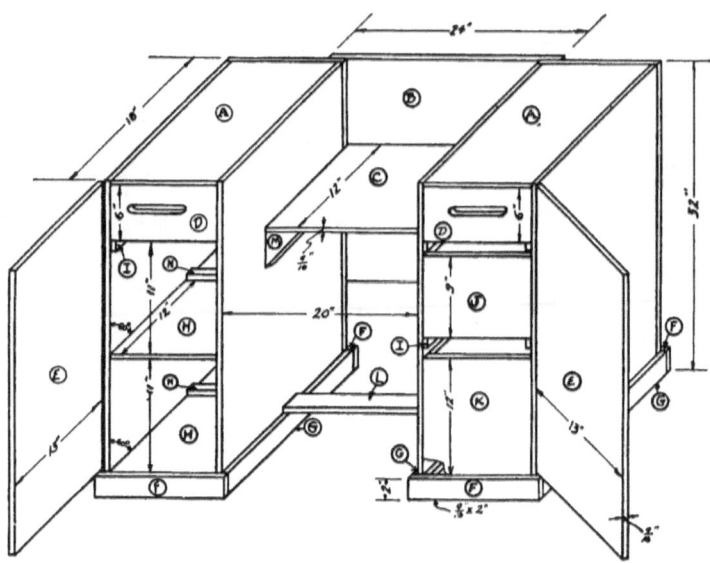

FIGURE 49.—*Vanity.*—Any girl would be proud of this vanity

for partitions L. One piece 5/16 by 12 by 30 3/16 inches for stocking tray bottom M. Eight butts (hinges). Heavy wire, for guides for polishing rag J.

Shape tops of ends A as shown in Figure 51. Nail back B and front strip C in place. Nail stocking tray bottom M to B and C. Secure partitions L in place. Next nail shoe cleats I to shelves H. Then nail shoe shelves in place at an angle of 68° with the vertical. Nail cleats K to ends A. Nail top half E to cleats K and back B. Bend wires J as shown and secure them to F. Hinge D and F to E. Hinge doors G to ends A.

In polishing the shoes, the foot is placed on F, and the polishing rag run under wires J and over the shoes.

VENTILATOR

One piece 7/16 by 14 inches by width of window A. Two pieces 1 1/16 by 5 by 10 inches, B.

Shape ends B as shown in Figure 52. Nail A to ends B. Ends B are then secured to inside of window frame.

LINEN CLOSET

Seven pieces 7/16 by 6 7/8 by 16 7/8 inches for shelves and top end A. One piece 5/16 by 12 by 33 inches for door B. Two pieces 5/16 by 3 by 33 inches, C. Two pieces 5/16 by 6 7/8 by 40 inches for sides D. One piece 3/4-inch doweling 18 inches in length for towel rod E. One piece 5/16 by 18 by 33 inches for back F. Two butts (hinges). One cupboard catch.

Shape bottom ends of sides D as shown in Figure 53, and bore 3/4-inch holes through them for towel rod E. Nail sides D and back F to top end of closet and shelves A. Nail front strips C in place. Hinge door B to C. Attach catch to door.

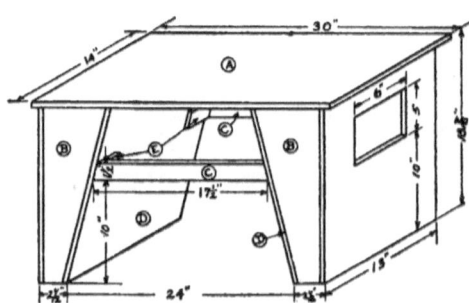

FIGURE 50.—*Vanity Bench.*—Of course this belongs with the vanity, but it can be used as a seat, besides

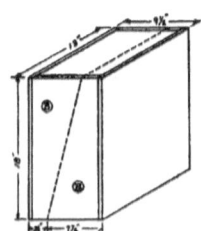

FIGURE 50A.—Illustrates how to cut box to form legs B of bench

PART II. INDOORS

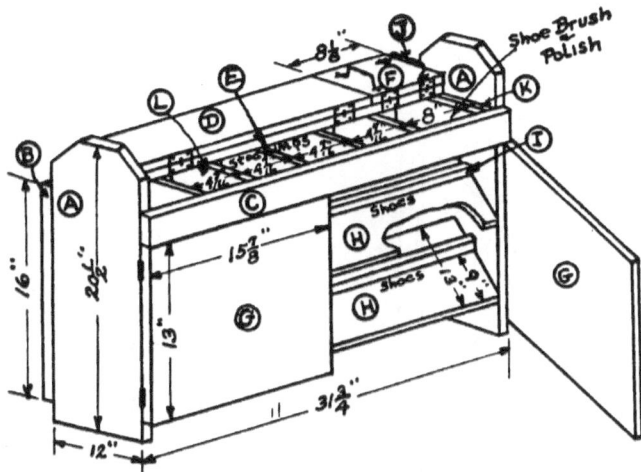

FIGURE 51.—*Bootery.*—For your shoes and stockings. A place for shoe polish and brush is also provided

BOOK AND MAGAZINE RACK

Two pieces 11/16 by 75/16 by 327/8 inches for ends *A*. One piece 11/16 by 341/4 by 36 inches for back *B*. Two pieces 11/16 by 75/16 by 36 inches for top and bottom, *C*. Two pieces 13/16 by 75/16 by 343/4 inches for shelves *D*. Four pieces 7/16 by 1 by 75/16 inches for shelf cleats *E*. One piece 9/16 by 133/4 by 345/8 inches for *F*. One piece 7/16 by 1 by 345/8 inches for *G*.

Nail top and bottom pieces *C* and back *B* to ends *A*. Nail shelf cleats *E* to the inside of ends *A* as shown in Figure 54. Nail strip *G* to bottom *C*. Place *F* so that the lower edge rests against *G*; it will be necessary to notch out the top ends to clear the bottom shelf cleats. Nail shelves *D* to cleats *E*.

WASTE-PAPER BASKET

A bushel basket covered with cretonne makes a handy, attractive waste-paper basket. (See fig. 55.)

DESK SET

One piece 11/16 by 8 by 9 inches for base *A*. One piece 11/16 by 5 by 8 inches for back *B*. One piece 11/16 by 31/2 by 8 inches for *C*.

Layout 13/4-inch square for inkwell, and round grooves for pen and pencil on base *A*. (See fig. 56.) A gouge should be used to cut the round grooves. Screw *B* to end of base *A*. Screw *C* to top face of base *A* 21/16 inches from *B*.

DESK BOOKCASE

One box 377/16 by 12 by 9 inches, *A*. One box 323/4 by 10 by 9 inches, *B*. One box 231/16 by 4 by 9 inches, *C*. One box 201/16 by 6 by 9 inches, *D*. One box 10 by 8 by 9 inches, *E*. One piece 11/16 inch by inside width by inside depth of box *D* for shelf *F*. Two pieces 11/16 inch by inside depth by inside width of box *B* for shelves *G*. Three pieces 11/16 inch by inside depth by inside width of box *A* for shelves *H*. One piece 11/16 inch by inside width by inside depth of box *C* for shelf *I*. One piece 11/16 inch by 9 by 40 inches for base *J*.

Remove top and one end from all boxes. Remove one side from boxes *B*, *C*, *D*, and *E* as shown in Figure 57. Secure shelves *F*, *G*, *H*, and *I* in boxes *D*, *B*, *A*, and *C*, respectively. Arrange boxes on their open ends on base *J* as shown, and nail them together.

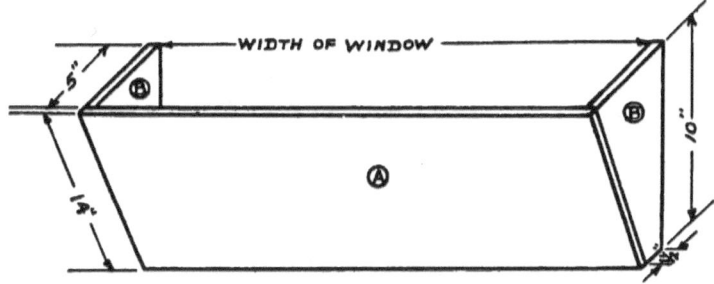

FIGURE 52.—*Ventilator.*—A ventilator in a window is often a real necessity

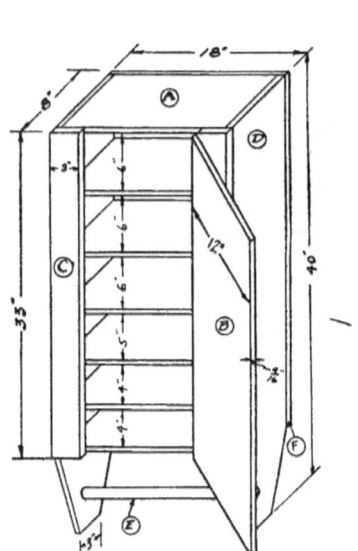

FIGURE 53.—*Linen Closet.*—A handy place for towels and similar supplies

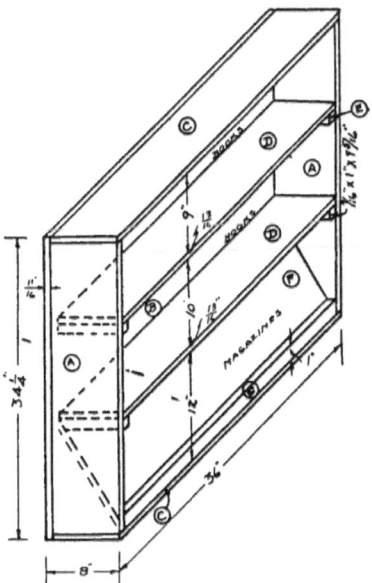

FIGURE 54.—*Book and Magazine Rack.*—Keeps the living room in order and preserves reading matter

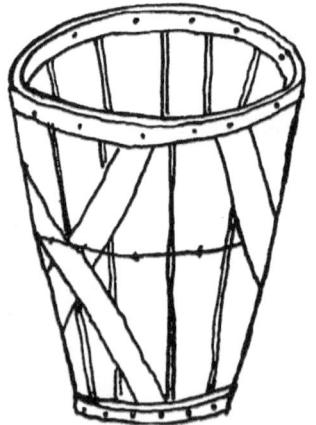

FIGURE 55.—*Waste-Paper Basket.*—Cover this with cretonne and you will have a neat, serviceable waste-paper receptacle

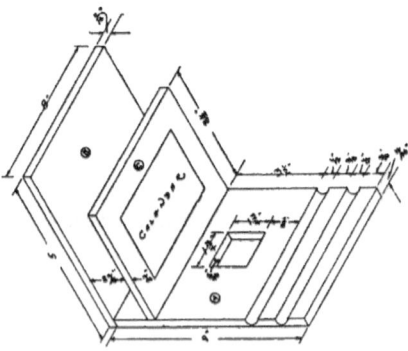

FIGURE 56.—*Desk Set.*—Provides a place for stationery, pens, and pencils

PART II. INDOORS 25

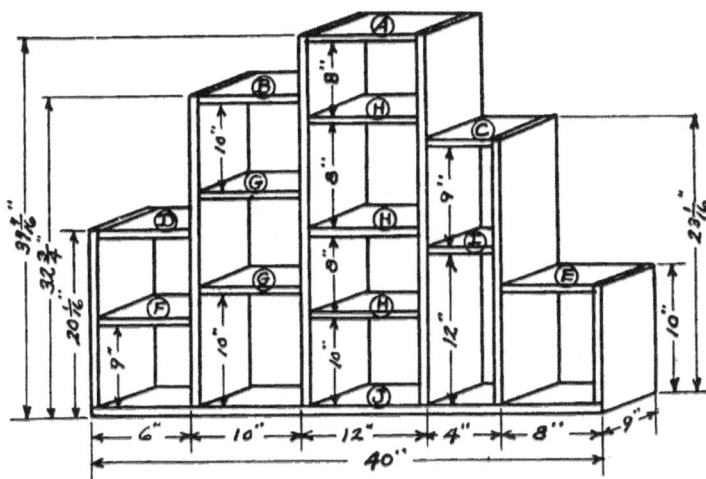

FIGURE 57.—*Desk Bookcase.*—Keep your library volumes in this futuristic bookcase

CORRESPONDENCE HOLDER

One piece 9/16 by 4¾ by 11⅜ inches, A. Two pieces 9/16 by 2 11/16 by 8 15/16 inches for ends B. One piece 9/16 by 3 by 12 inches for bottom C. One piece 9/16 by 6½ by 11⅜ inches for partition D. One piece 9/16 by 1 by 6½ inches for partition E. One piece 9/16 by 8 15/16 by 12 inches for back F. Two pieces 9/16 by 1 by 8 15/16 inches for partitions G.

Shape ends B as shown in Figure 58. Bevel edges of A and D. Construct holder by nailing pieces A, B, C, and F together as shown. Nail partition D in place. Shape ends of partitions E and G as shown and nail them in place between A and D, and D and F, respectively.

ADJUSTABLE BOOK ENDS

Two pieces 9/16 by 5 by 5¼ inches for ends A. One piece 9/16 by 5¼ by 18 inches for bottom B and C.

Shape ends A as shown in Figure 59. Cut the other piece to form B and C as shown. Then nail ends A to the wide ends of B and C.

DESK

One piece 1 1/16 by 26 by 45 inches for top A. Two boxes 29 by 24 by 11½ inches, B. Two pieces 9/16 by inside depth of box by 27 inches less thickness of one end of the box, for doors C. Four pieces 9/16 inch by inside depth of box by inside width of box less

9/16 inch for shelves D. Four pieces 9/16 by 2 by 24 inches, E. Four pieces 9/16 by 2 by 12⅝ inches, F. One piece 9/16 by 2½ by 20 inches, G. Four butts (hinges).

Remove one side from each of the boxes. Nail pieces E and F around one end of each box as shown in Figure 60. The bottom end of each of the boxes may be raised until the inner face is flush with the top edge of F. Secure shelves D in place in each of the boxes. Arrange boxes as shown, secure top A across the top ends of the boxes. Nail brace G to inside base strips E. Hinge doors C to boxes as shown.

TYPEWRITER STAND

One piece 25/32 by 17 by 30 inches for top A. Two pieces 25/32 by 16 3/16 by 28 inches for ends B. Two pieces 9/16 by 1 by 16 3/16 inches for cleats C. Two pieces 9/16 by 16 3/16 by 28 7/16 inches for shelves D. Two pieces 25/32 by 3 by 25 inches for feet E. One piece 25/32 by 3 by 31 9/16 inches for brace F. One piece 25/32 by 3 by 36 inches for diagonal brace G. Two pieces 9/16 by 1 13/16 by 16 3/16 inches for partitions H. One piece 25/32 by 4 5/16 by 30 inches for back brace I.

Nail top A to ends B as shown in Figure 61. Nail brace I to ends B, notice top A overlaps I. Cut off the corners of feet E as shown and nail them to ends B. Nail brace F across feet E as shown. Cut and nail diagonal brace G in place to ends B. Nail cleats C to the inside surfaces of ends B. Then nail shelves D and partitions H in place.

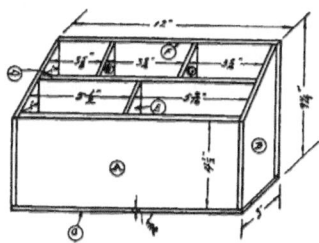

FIGURE 58.—*Correspondence Holder.*—A handy place for your writing paper and envelopes

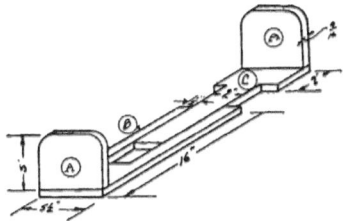

FIGURE 59.—*Adjustable Book Ends.*—Because this holder can be adjusted, one or a number of volumes may be kept in it

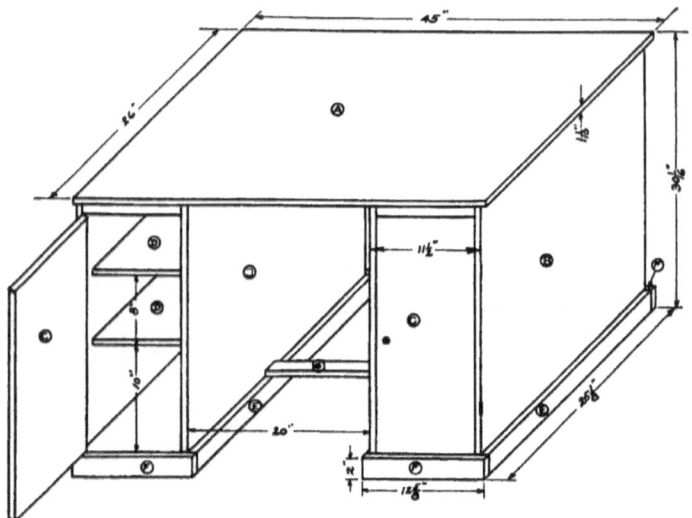

FIGURE 60.—*Desk.*—An invaluable piece of furniture for the camp or cottage

READING TABLE

One piece 25/32 by 24 by 32 inches for top A. Two boxes 24 by 8 by 10 inches, B. Two boxes 24 by 20 by 8 inches, C. Two pieces 9/16 by 5 by 20 inches, D. One piece 25/32 by 8 by 24 inches, E. One piece 9/16 by 16¼ inches by inside length of box C for F. One piece 9/16 inch by inside width by inside depth of box B for partition G. One piece 9/16 by 6 by 24 inches for H. One piece 25/32 by 2½ by 23 inches, I. One piece 9/16 by 4 by 24 inches, J. Two pieces 9/16 inch by inside depth by inside length of box C for shelves K. Four pieces 9/16 by 3 by 5 inches for cleats L. Two butts (hinges).

Remove one-half of one side of one box marked B. Nail partition G in place as shown in Figure 62. Remove one side of each of the boxes marked C. Cut out the ends and bottoms of boxes marked C as shown. Nail shelves K in one box marked C. Bevel edges of F and fasten it in place in the other box marked C. Shape pieces H and J alike, and secure them to boxes marked C as illustrated. Fasten boxes B and C together. Nail cleats L to sides of boxes B as shown. Nail pieces D to cleats L. Secure top A in place. Notch ends of I and secure to boxes C as shown. Hinge E to box B. Sewing or smoking equipment may be kept in box B at the right.

BOOKCASE SEAT

Two boxes 30 by 15¾ by 10 inches for ends A. One box 30 by 15 by 18 inches for seat F. One piece 1 1/16 by 12 by 30 inches for B. One piece 1 1/16 by 3¾ by 30 inches, C. Two pieces 7/16 by 10 by inside width of box A for doors D. Four pieces 1 1/16 by inside depth by inside width of boxes A for shelves E. Six butts (hinges).

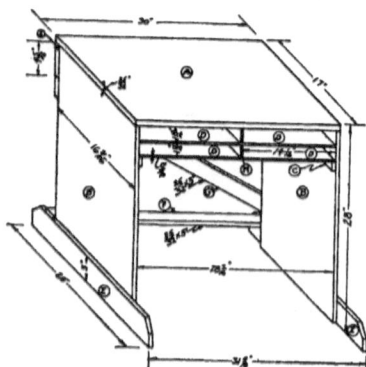

FIGURE 61.—*Typewriter Stand.*—For the camp typist

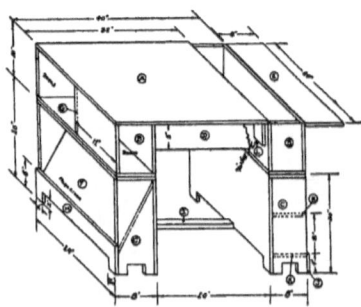

FIGURE 62.—*Reading Table.*—Books, magazines, and smoking equipment may be kept in this table

PART II. INDOORS

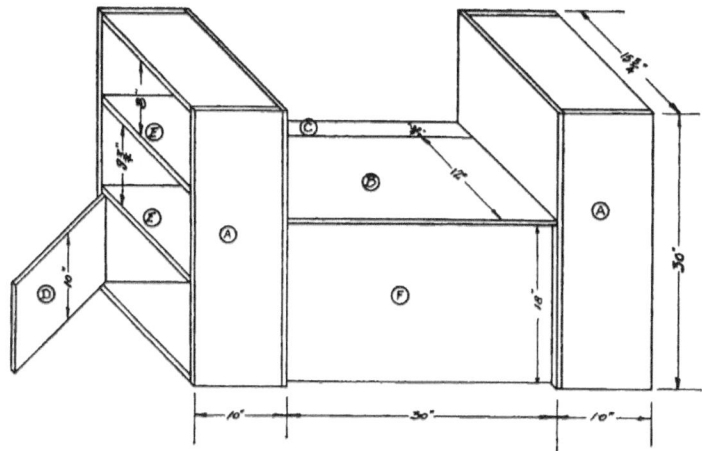

FIGURE 63.—*Bookcase Seat.*—This combination bookcase and seat covered with cretonne, will be a welcome addition to the camp living room

Secure shelves *E* in boxes *A* as shown in Figure 63. Nail *C* across the top of box *F*, as shown. Hinge *B* to *C*, the front edge of *B* will overlap front of *F* ¾ inch. Nail boxes *A* to *F*, as shown. Hinge doors *D* to lower part of *A*.

TABOURET

Two pieces 11/16 by 12 by 12 inches for *A*. Four pieces 11/16 by 3 by 19 inches for legs *B*.
Cut off the corners of *A* as shown in Figure 64. Then secure the legs to pieces marked *A* with round head wood screws.

DROP-LEAF TABLE

Two pieces 25/32 by 7 by 29 inches for legs *A*.
Two pieces 25/32 by 1½ by 13 inches for feet *B*.
One piece 25/32 by 3 by 23 inches for crossbar *C*.
Two pieces 25/32 by 8 by 29 inches for leaves *D*.

One piece 25/32 by 9 by 29 inches for top *E*. Two pieces 25/32 by 4¼ by 4¼ inches for brackets *F*. Eight butts (hinges).
Shape feet *B* as illustrated in Figure 65. Nail feet *B* to legs *A*. Secure top *E* to top ends of legs *A*; legs *A* should be spaced 23 inches apart. Nail crossbar *C* in place 3 inches from bottom ends of the legs *A*. Cut the two 4¼ inch square pieces diagonally across the ends, to form four triangular-shaped brackets *F*. Hinge brackets to top inside of legs *A*. Hinge leaves *D* to edges of top *E*.

COAT AND HAT RACK

One board 25/32 by 10 by 28 inches for top *A*. One board 25/32 by 12 by 28 inches for back *B*. One piece 25/32 by 8 by 8 inches for 2 braces *C*. Four pieces of broom handle 4¾ inches in length, *D*.
Lay out the centers of the four holes for sections of broom handle *D* on *B*, as shown in Figure 66

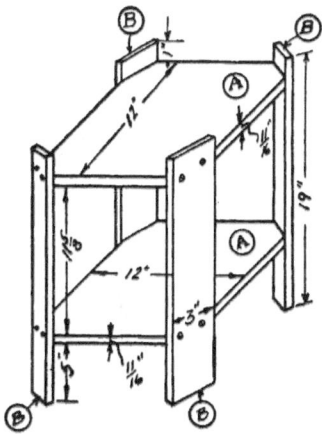

FIGURE 64.—*Tabouret.*—No camp is complete without this easily made tabouret

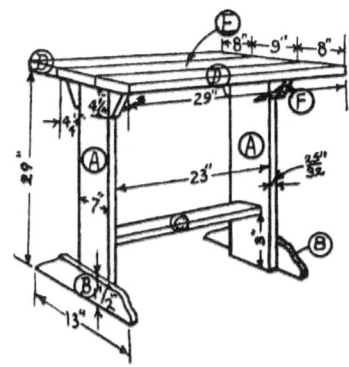

FIGURE 65.—*Drop-Leaf Table.*—A drop-leaf table is a real space saver

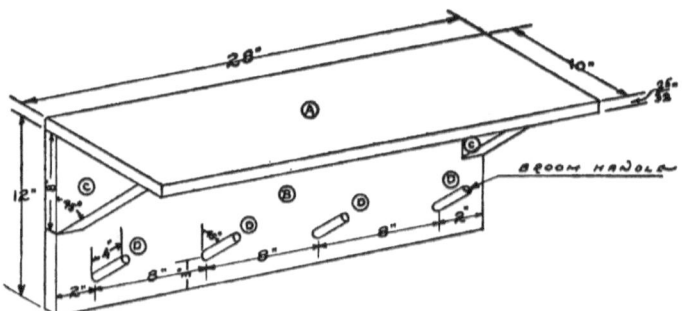

FIGURE 66.—*Coat and Hat Rack.*—This rack provides an easy way of keeping hats and coats in order

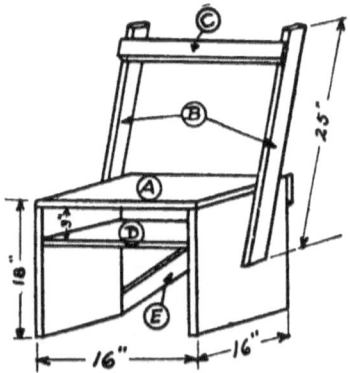

FIGURE 67.—*Chair.*—Waste wood turned into a chair. That seems to be an idea well worth a little work

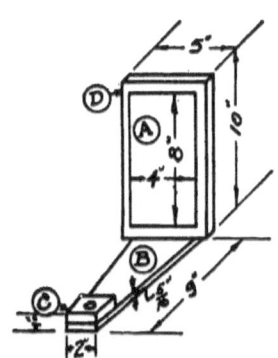

FIGURE 68.—*Sconce.*—A combination candle holder and reflector

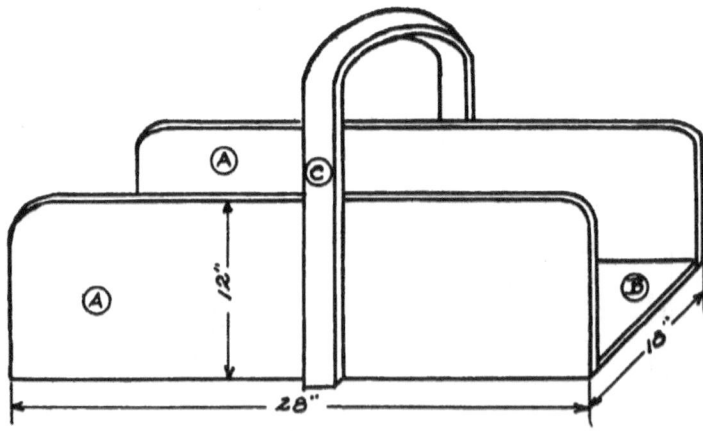

FIGURE 69.—*Fireplace Wood Basket.*—Complete your fireplace equipment with this wood basket

Bore these holes holding the bit at an angle of 45°. Glue pieces *D* in *B*. Coat hooks may be used. Nail *A* to *B* as shown. Cut the 8 by 8 inch square piece diagonally across the corners, forming two braces *C*. Nail these braces in place. The rack may be nailed or fastened to the wall with screws.

CHAIR

One box 18 by 16 by 16 inches, *A*. Two pieces 7/16 by 1¼ by 25 inches, *B*. One piece 7/16 by 2½ by 16⅞ inches, *C*. One piece 7/16 by 1¼ by 24½ inches for diagonal brace *E*.

Remove top, bottom, and one side from box *A*. Cut down side removed to make *D* so it will fit between the ends of *A* and nail it in place as shown in Figure 67. Pieces *B* and *C* should next be nailed together and then nailed to the ends of the box as shown. Nail diagonal brace *E* in place.

SCONCE

One piece shiny tin 4 by 8 inches for reflector *A*. One piece wood 9/16 by 4 by 9 inches, *B*. One piece 1 1/16 by 2¼ by 2¼ inches, *C*. One piece 9/16 by 5 by 10 inches, *D*.

Tack reflector *A* to *D* as shown in Figure 68. Glue or nail *C* to front end of *B*. Nail *B* to bottom end of *D*. A tin can, straightened, will supply the reflector material.

Cut *C* diagonally across the corners to form two triangular-shaped brackets, as shown in Figure 71. Nail brackets *C* to back *B*. Nail top *A* to *B* and brackets *C*.

WINDOW SEAT

Two pieces 25/32 by 3¼ by 17½ inches for arm rests *A*. Four pieces 1 1/16 by 1 13/16 by 29¼ inches for leg pieces *B*. Four pieces 1 1/16 by 2½ by 29¼ inches for leg pieces *C*. Two pieces 1 1/16 by 4 by 31 inches for facing strips *D*. Two pieces 1 1/16 by 4 by 11 inches for facing strips *E*. Six pieces 1 1/16 by 2½ by 14⅝ inches for *F*, *I*, and *J*. One piece 1 1/16 by 2½ by 34⅝ inches for *G*. Two pieces 1 1/16 by 2½ by 33¼ inches for *H*. One piece (may consist of two or three boards) 1 1/16 by 14⅝ by 34⅝ inches, *K*. One piece 1 1/16 by 2½ by 13¼ inches for center brace *L*.

Construct four legs from pieces *B* and *C*, as shown in Figure 72. Secure pieces *F*, *I*, and *J* to leg strips *B*. Secure seat supports *H* and *I* to leg strips *C* and *B*, respectively. Nail center support *L* to seat supports *H*. Nail seat boards *K* to supports *H* and *I*. Nail *G* to upper edges of end strips *F*. Secure facing strips *D* and *E* to seat supports *H* and *I*. Secure arm rests *A* across top ends of legs. A seat cushion of layers of felt, or any preferred stuffing, is easily made.

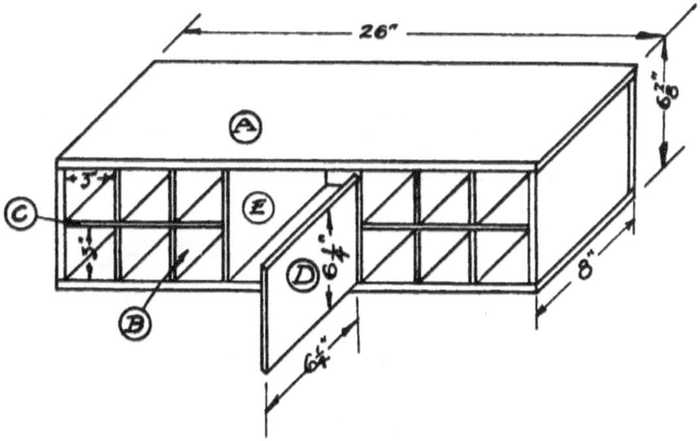

FIGURE 70.—*Desk Filing Cabinet.*—Will fit on any type of desk

FIREPLACE WOOD BASKET

Two pieces 9/16 by 12 by 28 inches for sides *A*. One piece 9/16 by 16⅞ by 28 inches for bottom *B*. One wood barrel hoop for handle *C*.

Round corners of *A* as shown in Figure 69. Nail sides *A* to bottom *B*. Nail barrel-hoop handle to the sides and edges of the bottom as shown.

DESK FILING CABINET

One box 26 by 8 by 6⅞ inches, *A*. Eight pieces 3/16 by 3 by inside width of box *A* for partitions *B*. Two pieces 3/16 by inside width of box *A* by 9⅝ inches, *C*. One piece 5/16 by 6¼ by 6¼ inches for door *D*. Two pieces 3/16 by 6 3/16 by inside width of box for *E*. Two butts (hinges) and one catch.

Remove one side of box. Replace top. Secure center partitions *E* in place as shown in Figure 70. Nail partitions *C* to ends of box and partitions *E*. Fasten partitions *D* between *C* and top and bottom of box.

SHELF

One piece 25/32 by 8 by 26 inches, *A*. One piece 25/32 by 8½ by 26 inches, *B*. One piece 25/32 by 6¼ by 6¼ inches, *C*.

BRACKET

One box, any size. Two facing strips 7/16 inch in thickness for *C*. One facing strip 7/16 inch in thickness for *B*.

Cut the box diagonally through the sides, as shown in Figure 73. Nail facing strips *C* over the protruding sides of the box section. Nail *B* across the top of the protruding ends of back *A*.

BREAKFAST TABLE AND CABINET

Two pieces 1 1/16 by 10 5/16 by 40 inches for sides *A*. One piece 1 1/16 by 30 by 40 inches for back *B*. One piece 1 1/16 by 10 5/16 by 28⅝ inches for top shelf *C*. Four pieces 1 1/16 by 9⅝ by 28⅝ inches for shelves *D*. Ten pieces 1 1/16 by 1⅜ by 9⅝ inches for shelf cleats *E*. One piece 1 1/16 by 28⅝ by 37 5/16 inches for table top *F*. Two pieces 1 1/16 by 1¾ by 28 inches for legs *G*. One piece 1 1/16 by 1¾ by 26 inches for cleat *H*. One piece 1 1/16 by 1¾ by 22½ inches for cleat *I*. Four butts (hinges).

Round off top front corners of sides *A* as shown in Figure 74. Nail shelf cleats *E* to the inside of sides *A*. The rear end of the cleats should be flush with the rear edges of sides *A*. Nail shelf *C* and shelves

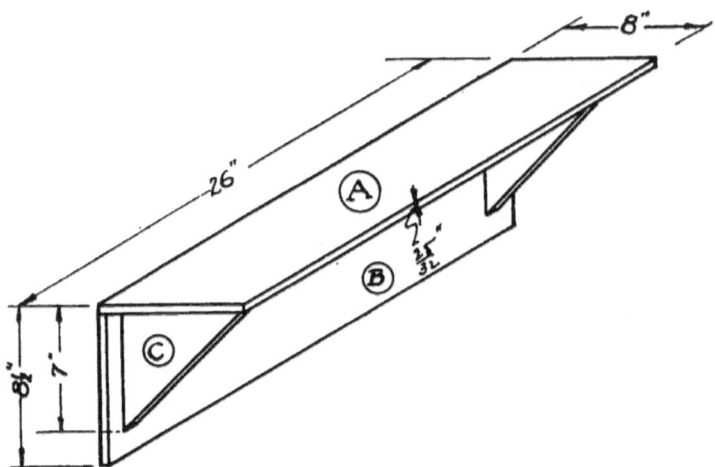

FIGURE 71.—*Shelf.*—You can not have too many shelves in your cabin or cottage

D to cleats. The front edge of top shelf C will be flush with the front edges of sides A, while the front edges of shelves D will be $1\frac{1}{16}$ inch in from front edge of sides A, so table top F, when closed up, will fit in between sides A and directly under top shelf C. Nail back B to sides A. Construct table top F by cleating together boards to make up top with cleats H and I as shown. Hinge legs G to cleats H as shown. Hinge table F to bottom shelf D so that the top end of F will come directly under top shelf C; the bottom end of F should then be flush with the bottom ends of sides A. Chains or metal guides should be used to keep legs from swinging past a vertical position when the table is lowered.

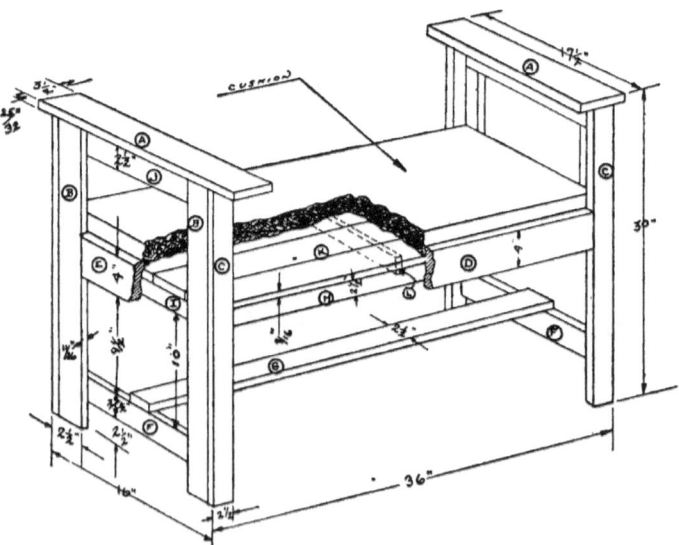

FIGURE 72.—*Window Seat.*—When quite a lot of visitors drop in a window seat is mighty handy

PART II. INDOORS

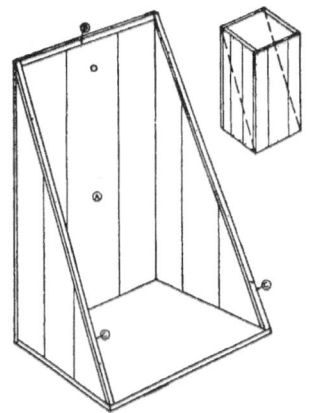

FIGURE 73.—*Bracket.*—One box will supply the wood for a pair of these brackets

FIGURE 74.—*Breakfast Table and Cabinet.*—As a space saver, anywhere, this is a fine idea

WINDOW FLYTRAP

Two pieces 9/16 by 10⅞ by 22⅞ inches for ends A. One piece 9/16 by 10⅞ inches by width of window for top B. Two pieces 9/16 by 2 inches by width of window for strips C. One piece 9/16 by 5 7/16 inches by width of window for D. One piece 9/16 by 3 7/17 inches by width of window for E. One piece 9/16 by 12 by width of window for F. Two pieces 9/16 by 1 by 7 7/16 inches for cleats G. Four pieces 9/16 by 1 by 9½ inches for cleats H. Four pieces 9/16 by 1 by 6½ inches for cleats I. Two pieces 9/16 by 1 by 5¼ inches for cleats J. Two pieces 9/16 by 1 by 3 7/16 inches for cleats L. Two pieces 9/16 by 1 by 10¼ inches for cleats M. Two pieces 9/16 by 1 by 5 7/16 inches for cleats N. Two pieces 9/16 by 1 by 3 7/16 inches for cleats P. Three pieces 9/16 by 1 inch by width of window for strips R. Wire screen cloth. Two butts (hinges). Two hooks and eyes.

In constructing the window flytrap shown in Figure 75 follow the illustrations closely. Shape the screening, and cut the notches in the creases as shown in Figure 75a. The width of the screening should be such as to permit the ends to overlap the cleats nailed to trap ends A as shown in Figure 75. Cut ends of cleats H, M, N, and P as shown in

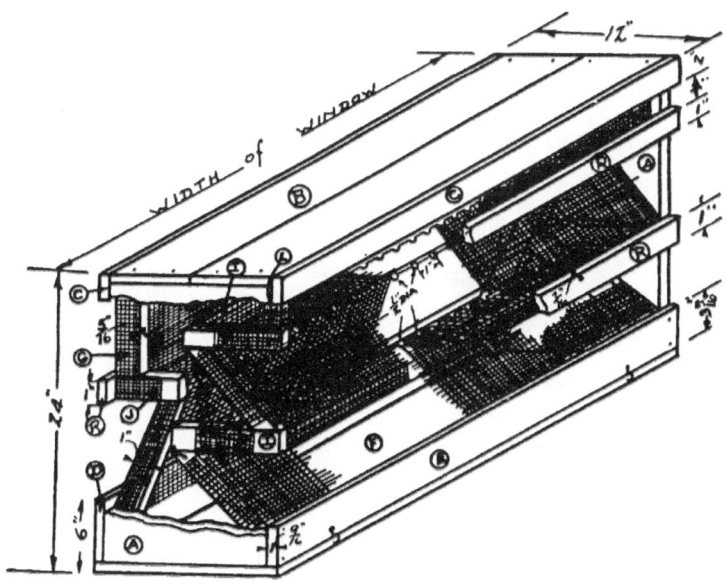

FIGURE 75.—*Windowfly Trap.*—This looks more complicated to make than it really is. Courtesy United States Department of Agriculture

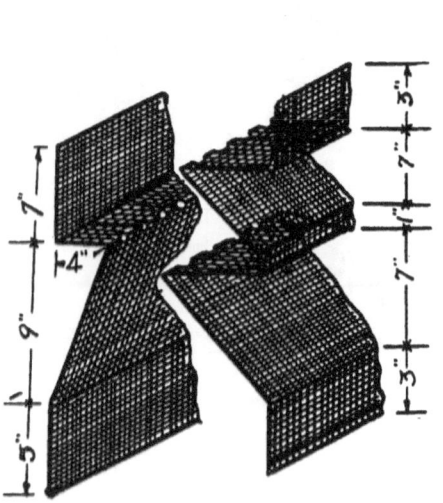

FIGURE 75A.—Shows screen details

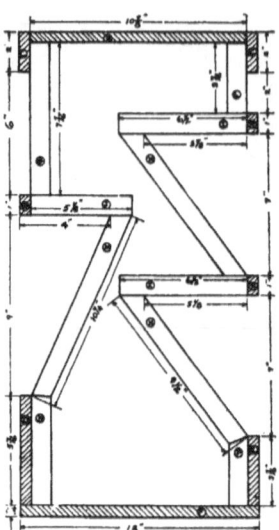

FIGURE 75B.—End of trap with end board removed, showing arrangement of cleats holding wire screening in place.

Figure 75b, which shows the arrangement of the cleats with end A of the trap removed. Nail the screening to cross cleats R, then nail these cleats to trap ends A. Nail cross cleats C to trap ends A, then secure screening to these cleats. Nail cleats G, J, M, N, L, I, H, and P to trap ends A, to hold overlapping ends of wire screening securely in place. Nail top B to trap ends A. Nail crosspieces D and E to ends A. Bottom F is hinged to D. Place in open window and close sash on it. Flies are trapped going in or out.

KNIFE, FORK, AND SPOON TRAY

Two pieces 9/16 by 2 7/16 by 9 inches for ends A. Two pieces 9/16 by 2 7/16 by 12 7/8 inches for sides B. One piece 9/16 by 2 7/16 by 7 7/8 inches, C. One piece 9/16 by 3 3/4 by 9 9/16 inches for handle D. One piece 9/16 by 9 by 14 inches for bottom E.

Nail ends A, sides B, and bottom E together as shown in Figure 76. Nail partition C in place between sides B. Shape D as shown and nail it between A and C.

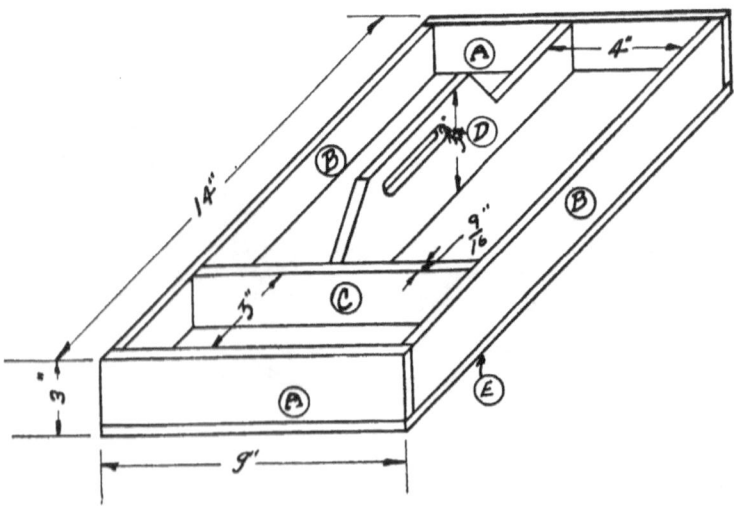

FIGURE 76.—*Knife, Fork, and Spoon Tray.*—Keep your knives, forks, and spoons separated

PART II. INDOORS

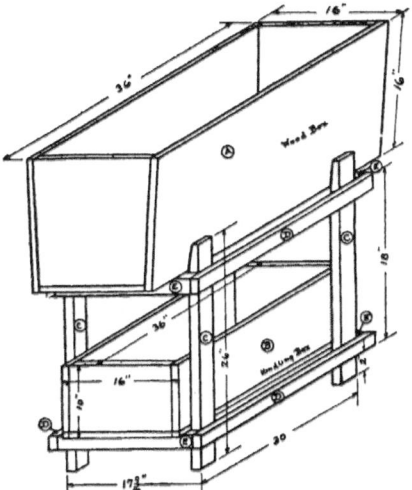

FIGURE 77.—*Elevated Wood Box.*—Both logs and kindling may be kept in this box

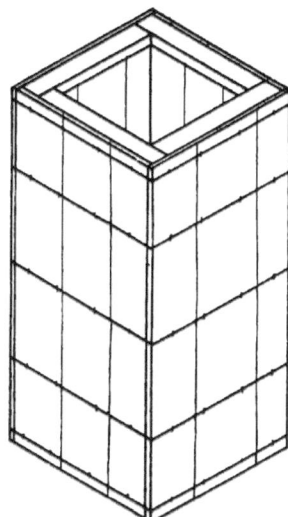

FIGURE 78.—*Trash Receptacle.*—An easily made trash holder

ELEVATED WOOD BOX

One box 36 by 16 by 16 inches for wood box A. One box 36 by 16 by 10 inches for kindling box B. Four pieces $2\frac{5}{32}$ by $1\frac{1}{2}$ by 26 inches for legs C. Four pieces $2\frac{5}{32}$ by $1\frac{1}{4}$ by $31\frac{9}{16}$ inches for side braces D. Four pieces $2\frac{5}{32}$ by $1\frac{1}{4}$ by $17\frac{9}{16}$ inches for end braces E.

Nail end braces E to narrow edges of legs C, as shown in Figure 77. Nail side braces D to legs C and to ends of E. The boxes fit on the framework as shown.

TRASH RECEPTACLE

Wire-bound and plywood boxes make excellent trash receptacles. Simply knock in one end. (See fig. 78.)

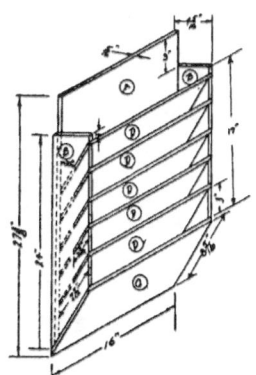

FIGURE 79.—*Pan Lid Rack.*—This is essentially for the cook's convenience

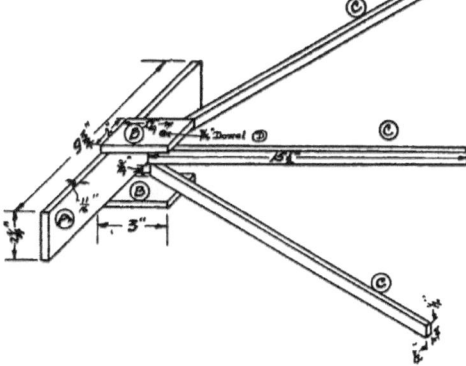

FIGURE 80.—*Towel Rack.*—Do not ruin your towels by hanging them on nails

PAN-LID RACK

One piece $\frac{5}{16}$ by $15\frac{3}{8}$ by $27\frac{1}{16}$ inches for back A. Two pieces $\frac{5}{16}$ by $4\frac{9}{16}$ by 24 inches for ends B. One piece $\frac{5}{16}$ by $8\frac{5}{16}$ by 16 inches for bottom C. Five pieces $\frac{5}{16}$ by $7\frac{1}{2}$ by 16 inches for partitions D.

Shape ends B as shown in Figure 79. Then cut five slots at an angle of 30° with the vertical, as shown. These slots should be cut $3\frac{3}{4}$ inches deep, one-half the width of partitions D. Then cut a piece $3\frac{3}{4}$ inches long, $\frac{5}{16}$ inch wide from each end of partitions D. Nail sides B to A. Nail bottom C in place. Slip partitions D in place in the notches in sides B. The rack may be hung on the wall or secured to the inside of a cabinet door.

TOWEL RACK

One piece $1\frac{1}{16}$ by 2 by $9\frac{3}{4}$ inches, A. Two pieces $1\frac{1}{16}$ by 2 by 3 inches, B. Three pieces $2\frac{5}{32}$ by $2\frac{5}{32}$ by $15\frac{1}{4}$ inches, C. One piece $\frac{7}{16}$ inch doweling $3\frac{3}{4}$ inches in length, D.

Bore a $\frac{7}{16}$-inch hole through pieces marked B as shown in Figure 80. Nail pieces marked B to A as shown. Shape pieces C by tapering one end down to $\frac{1}{2}$ by $\frac{1}{2}$ inch, then bore a $\frac{7}{16}$-inch hole through the large end of all three about $\frac{1}{2}$ inch from their ends. Dowel the sticks together as shown.

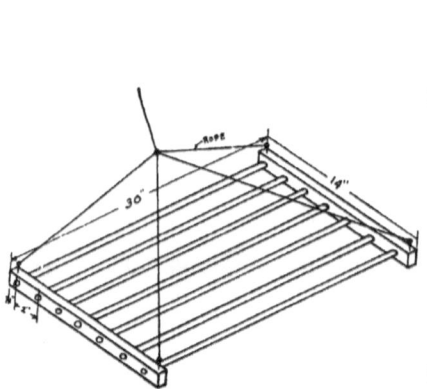

FIGURE 81.—*Clothes Drier.*—Suspended from the ceiling this keeps drying garments out of the way

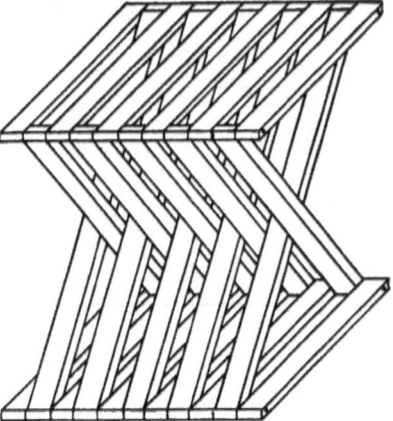

FIGURE 82.—*Stool.*—Always useful, easily moved about, and not difficult to make

CLOTHES DRIER

Two pieces 1 1/16 by 1 1/4 by 14 inches for ends. Seven 1/2-inch dowels 30 inches long.

Through the two end pieces bore seven 1/2-inch holes as shown in Figure 81. Glue the ends of the dowels in the end pieces as shown. A thin brad driven through each end of the dowels in the end pieces will help to keep them in place. This clothes drier is to be suspended by ropes run through pulleys in the ceiling, directly over a stove or register.

STOOL

One 1-bushel onion crate.

Remove bottom from crate. Remove two corner wires from ends of crates, so the pieces of one side come loose. Reverse one end of the crate, and replace the side strips as shown in Figure 82. In some cases it will be necessary to force these strips into place. Replace the corner wires that were removed.

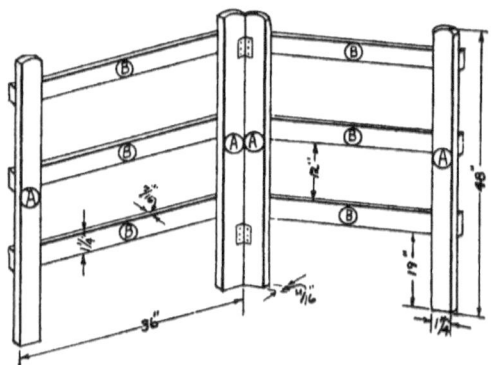

FIGURE 83.—*Clotheshorse.*—A wash day necessity

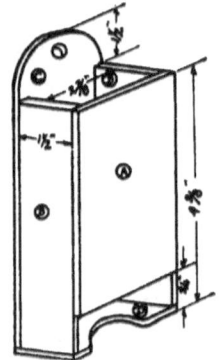

FIGURE 84.—*Safety-match Box Holder.*—Just as easy to make as it looks.

CLOTHESHORSE

Four pieces 1 1/16 by 1 1/4 by 48 inches for legs *A*. Six pieces 3/16 by 1 1/4 by 36 inches for cross strips *B*. Two butts (hinges).

Round off the top ends of legs *A*, as shown in Figure 83. Nail cross strips *B* to legs *A*. Hinge the two sections together.

SAFETY-MATCH-BOX HOLDER

One piece 3/16 by 2 3/4 by 3 5/8 inches, *A*. Two pieces 3/16 by 1 1/2 by 4 3/16 inches for ends *B*. One piece 3/16 by 3 by 5 11/16 inches for back *C*. One piece 3/16 by 2 by 3 inches for bottom *D*.

Shape back *C* and bottom *D* as shown in Figure 84. Nail *A* and *C* to ends *B*. Nail bottom *D* in place.

PART II. INDOORS

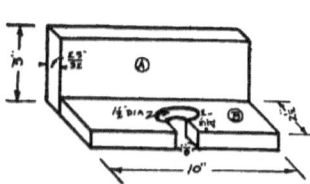

FIGURE 85.—*Broom Holder.*—Another article the camp housekeeper will appreciate

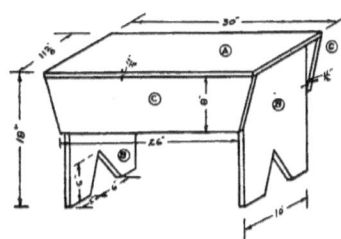

FIGURE 86.—*Bench.*—A well-made bench has many uses and serves many purposes

BROOM HOLDER

One piece 25/32 by 3 by 10 inches for *A*. One piece 25/32 by 2½ by 10 inches for *B*.

Bore 1½-inch diameter hole through the center of *B*. Cut an opening from hole through to front edge of *B*. Nail *A* securely to *B*. (See fig. 85.)

BENCH

One piece 11/16 by 11⅜ by 30 inches for top *A*. Two pieces 11/16 by 10 by 17 5/16 inches for ends *B*. Two pieces 11/16 by 8 by 30 inches for side braces *C*.

Cut grooves in bench ends *B*. Cut ends of side braces *C* as shown in Figure 86. Nail top *A* to top ends *B*; ends of *A* will overlap 2 inches. Nail side braces *C* to ends *B*. Nail top to side braces *C*.

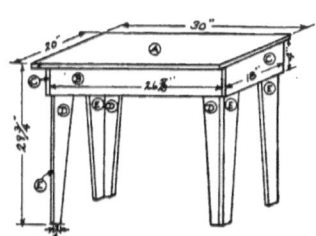

FIGURE 87.—*Kitchen Table.*—A positive necessity and should be built substantially to withstand wear and tear

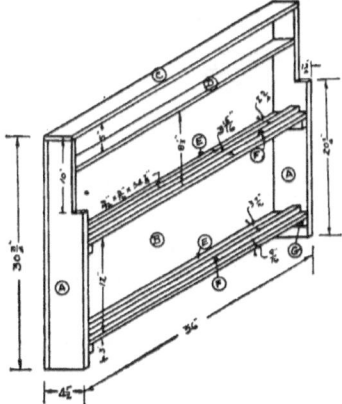

FIGURE 88.—*Wall Plate Rack.*—Easily constructed, useful, and can be made attractive

KITCHEN TABLE

One piece 25/32 by 20 by 30 inches for top *A*. Two pieces 11/16 by 4 by 26⅝ inches, *B*. Two pieces 11/16 by 4 by 18 inches, *C*. Four pieces 11/16 by 1¾ by 29 inches for leg strips *D*. Four pieces 11/16 by 2 7/16 by 29 inches for leg strips *E*.

Nail pieces *B* and *C* together as shown in Figure 87. Shape leg strips *D* and *E* as shown; *D* should be 1¾ inches wide at one end and ¾ inch at the other end; *E* should be 2 7/16 inches wide at one end and 1 7/16 inches at the other. Nail leg strips *D* and *E* together; then secure the legs just formed in the corners of the framework by nailing *B* and *C* together. Fasten top *A* to *B* and *C*. The top may be covered with sheet metal or porcelain, or it may be painted and varnished with valspar.

WALL PLATE RACK

Two pieces 9/16 by 3 15/16 by 30 3/16 inches for ends *A*. One piece 9/16 by 30 3/16 by 36 inches for back *B*. One piece 9/16 by 2¾ by 36 inches for top *C*. One piece 9/16 by 2 3/16 by 34⅞ inches for top shelf *D*. Two pieces 11/16 by 3 15/16 by 34⅞ inches for shelves *E*. Two strips 3/16 by 9/16 by 34⅞ inches for plate cleats *F*. Four pieces 9/16 by 1 by 3 15/16 inches for shelf cleats *G*.

Shape ends *A* as shown in Figure 88. Nail back *B* to ends *A*. Nail top *C* to upper ends of *A*. Cleats *G* and top shelf *D* should also be nailed to ends *A*. Nail strips *F* to shelves *E*, which should then be nailed to cleats *G*.

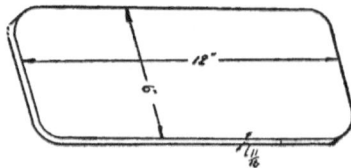

FIGURE 89.—*Meat or Bread Board.*—Saves knives as well as table tops

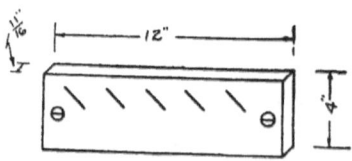

FIGURE 90.—*Fishing-Pole Rack.*—This rack is convenient for either one or several poles.

MEAT OR BREAD BOARD

One piece hardwood 1 1/16 by 6 by 12 inches. Shape board as shown in Figure 89. Rub down with oil, and paint with valspar.

FISHING-POLE RACK

One piece 1 1/16 by 4 by 12 inches.
Drive five nails in the block as shown in Figure 90. The poles should be hung in a vertical position, by hooking the pole tips over the nails.

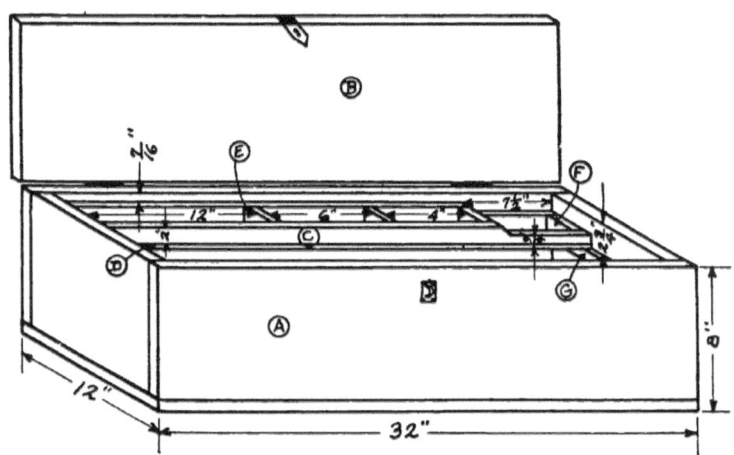

FIGURE 91.—*Tool Chest.*—Skillfully made, a tool chest should last a lifetime

TOOL CHEST

One box 32 by 12 by 8 inches, A. One piece 1 1/16 by 12 by 32 inches for lid B. Two pieces 9/16 by 2 inches by inside length of box A for tray sides C. One piece 9/16 by 6 inches by inside length of box A for tray bottom D. Four pieces 9/16 by 2 by 5 5/8 inches for partitions E and end of tray. One piece 9/16 by 3/4 by 5 5/8 inches for tray end F. Two pieces 9/16 by 1 inch by inside width of box A for cleats G. Two butts (hinges). One hinge hasp and lock.

Shape tray sides C as shown in Figure 91. Nail sides C, end F, partitions E, and bottom D together to construct tray. Nail cleats G to ends of box A, as shown. Hinge lid B to box.

PART II. INDOORS

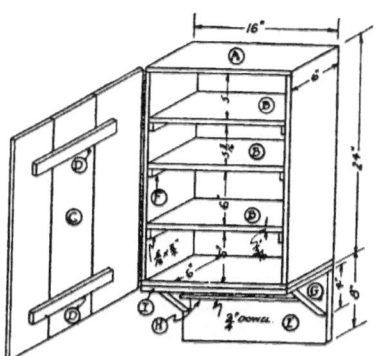

FIGURE 92.—*Bathroom Cabinet.*—If you have a bathroom cabinet make this for your own room

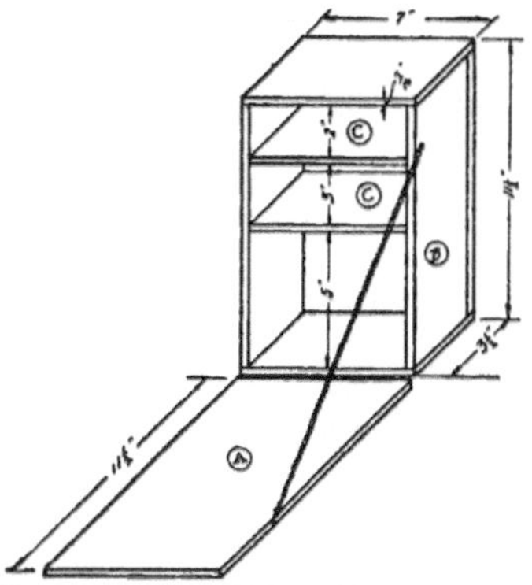

FIGURE 93.—*First-Aid Box.*—No camp should be without a first-aid box

BATHROOM CABINET

One box 24 by 16 by 6 inches, A. Three pieces ⁵⁄₁₆ by inside depth by inside width of box for shelves B. One piece ⁷⁄₁₆ by 16 by 24 inches for door C. Two pieces ⁵⁄₁₆ by ¾ by 12 inches for cleats D. One piece ¹¹⁄₁₆ by 8 by 16 inches for shelf back E. Six pieces ⁵⁄₁₆ by ¾ by inside depth of box for shelf cleats F. One piece ¹¹⁄₁₆ by 4 by 4 inches for brackets G. One piece ¾-inch doweling 16 inches in length for towel rod H. One piece ¹¹⁄₁₆ by 6 by 16 inches for shelf top I. Two butts (hinges) and snap.

Nail cleats F to sides of box as shown in Figure 92. Nail shelves B to cleats F. If door is to be built up of several boards, cleat them together with cleats D as shown. Cut G diagonally across the corners to form triangular-shaped brackets. Bore ¾-inch hole through brackets. Construct shelf as shown from pieces I, E, and G. Insert rod E in holes in brackets G. Hinge door C to box A. Secure cabinet to shelf which in turn is fastened to the wall. If desired, a mirror may be fitted to front of door.

FIRST-AID BOX

One piece ⁷⁄₁₆ by 7 by 11½ inches for door A. One box 11½ by 7 by 3½ inches, B. Two pieces ⁵⁄₁₆ by inside depth by inside width of box B for shelves C. Two butts (hinges). Light chain.

Nail shelves C in box as shown in Figure 93. Hinge door A to bottom end of box. A chain may be used to keep the door in a horizontal position when open. The door then acts as a table. The box may be secured to a tree or the wall of the cabin or cottage.

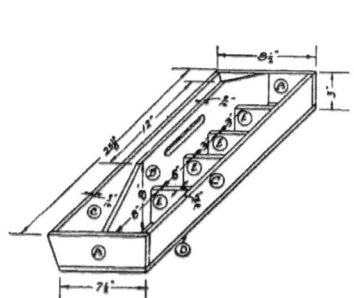

FIGURE 94.—*Portable Tool Box.*—Tools may may be conveniently carried from place to place in this box

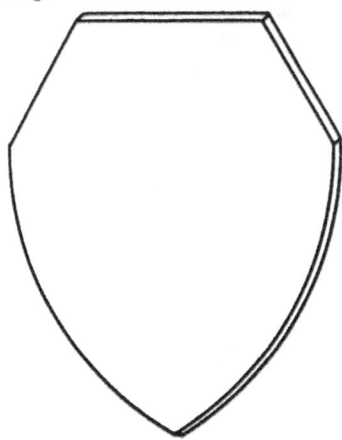

FIGURE 95.—*Head Mounting Board.*—For mounting your finest trophies

PORTABLE TOOL BOX

Two pieces ⁹⁄₁₆ by 2⁷⁄₁₆ by 8½ inches for ends A. One piece ⁹⁄₁₆ by 8 by 24 inches, B. Two pieces ⁹⁄₁₆ by 2⁷⁄₁₆ by 24 inches for sides C. One piece ⁹⁄₁₆ by 7½ by 25¼ inches for bottom D. Four pieces ⁹⁄₁₆ by 2⁷⁄₁₆ by 3¾ inches for partitions E.

Shape ends A as shown in Figure 94. Construct box by nailing ends A, sides C, and bottom D together. Shape handle B as shown and secure it to ends A and bottom D. Secure partitions E in place, nailing them to C and B.

HEAD MOUNTING BOARD

The size of the mounting board will naturally depend on what is to be mounted. Lumber 1 1/16 inch in thickness is suggested for use, in most cases. (See fig. 95.)

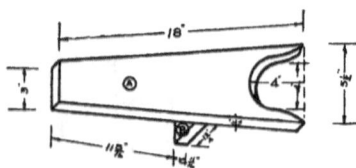

FIGURE 96.—*Bootjack.*—To help remove boots and shoes

FIGURE 97.—*Necktie Rack.*—Can be painted to match any color scheme

BOOTJACK

One piece 1 1/16 by 5 1/2 by 18 inches for *A*. One piece 1 1/16 by 1 3/4 by 4 1 1/16 inches for *B*.
Shape *A* as shown in Figure 96. Secure *B* to the underside of *A*.

NECKTIE RACK

One piece 9/16 by 4 by 14 inches, *A*. One piece 5/16 by 3/4 by 12 inches, *B*. Two pieces 7/16 by 3/4 by 3/4 inches, *C*.
Nail *B* and pieces marked *C* to *A* as shown in Figure 97.

APPENDIX

PREVENT FOREST FIRES

By R. Y. STUART [1]

"Fire is a good servant, but a bad master."

Woods fires in the United States cause millions of dollars worth of damage to mature timber, young growth, and other property every year. They destroy the little trees in the forest that should be the big trees of the future, they destroy the feathered and furry inhabitants of the woods, they prevent the forests from giving full protection to watersheds, and they ruin choice scenic areas and camp grounds.

And most of these fires are preventable. Individual responsibility, cooperation, and good sense, must therefore be depended upon in the struggle of use against abuse of fire.

According to the records of the United States Forest Service, careless smokers and campers are responsible for nearly one-third of the fires in the forests. These records of forests under protection place the major responsibility on human agencies; therefore greater care must be taken with matches, pipe ashes, and cigar and cigarette stubs, because they are the chief sources of fire in the forests. Be sure your match is out; break it in two before you throw it away, is one good rule in outdoor good manners. Be sure that pipe ashes and cigar and cigarette stubs are dead before throwing them away; above all, never throw them into brush, leaves, or needles, is another. Last, but not least: If you come across a fire already let loose, even if you are not responsible or may be in a hurry, be a good enough sport to put it out. If water is not at hand, try earth, particularly damp sand; and if the fire has gained too much headway for you to fight single-handed or with what help you have, get help—find the forest ranger or some near-by farmer. Don't stop until the fire is down and out.

CAMP FIRE COMFORT AND CAUTION

Many people have a sense of "good woodsmanship" in the matter of selecting a safe place in which to build the fire that will cook the day's appetizing meals, and around which will center the evening pastime. There are, however, others who know the "why," but not the "how" and "where" of the camp fire. In one year, 3,681 camp fires in the National Forest were so carelessly built or tended that they "got away," burned over 275,860 acres, and caused damage totaling thousands of dollars.

BUILDING THE CAMP FIRE

Some one has said that "nothing betrays the tenderfoot sooner than his fire. The woodsman builds a small, quick fire, sits beside it, and does his cooking. The tenderfoot makes a bonfire and cooks himself, while he smokes and burns his food."

An experienced camper never builds his fire near living trees, dead logs, or underbrush. He keeps away from overhanging branches and picks a good open space. He always builds it on an earth or rock foundation, scraping away all inflammable material—grass, needles, and trash—within a radius of 3 to 5 feet.

---

[1] Forester, U. S. Forest Service, Department of Agriculture, and vice chairman, National Committee on Wood Utilization.

Then he may dig a small hole to lay the fire in, and place a rock on each side. A few iron rods, about 3 feet long, to be laid across a fire, are a useful addition to the camp outfit. Many convenient and useful types of camp grills and stoves, of course, are on the market.

If the wind comes up strongly, keep the fire small or put it out entirely.

Every one who builds open fires should be equipped with a shovel, ax, and water bucket, to assist in putting out as well as in building the fire and cooking the meal.

THE RIGHTEOUS END OF A USEFUL FIRE

When breaking camp, the fire should be put out, dead out. Most States have laws requiring this and it is good woodsmanship. Use water or earth. Drench the fire thoroughly, and stir the embers while pouring on water so that the last spark will be killed, with no chance of coming to life again. It is best to top off with a shovelful of earth, for good measure.

FIGURE 98.—*Camp Fire Correctly Built.*—The experienced woodsman builds a small camp fire in a safe place. Courtesy United States Forest Service

FIGURE 99.—*Camp Fire Correctly Extinguished.*—And drowns it with water before he leaves. Courtesy United States Forest Service

WHAT NOT TO DO

Never build a fire against a log or stump.

Never build a camp fire near brush or dry grass. The wind may carry it beyond control in a few seconds.

Never build a fire against a tree. Even if the fire does not scorch the foliage, it will dry out the bark and injure the growth.

Never leave a camp fire untended, even for a few minutes. A sudden wind may cause it to do the unexpected thing.

Never leave a camp ground until you are perfectly sure that the camp fire is out, dead out.

ATTRACTING BIRDS [1]

The fact that birds feed on practically all insect pests and are instrumental in destroying weeds also, would make their presence desirable even without their beautiful coloring and lovely songs.

A simple way to attract, enjoy, and enlist the services of these friendly little creatures is to provide them with suitable and convenient ready-made homes.

---

[1] Information from Homes for Birds, Farmer's Bull. No. 1456, U. S. Department of Agriculture.

To be satisfactory, bird houses should be well-built, durable, cool, rain-proof, and accessible, since they should be cleaned after each brood's departure. Painting the houses increases their resistance to weather and adds to their attractiveness—brown, gray, and dull green are preferred colors for painting.

The roof of a bird house should slope sufficiently to shed water, or should have a groove cut across the face of the overhanging part. It should overhang the entrance by 2 or 3 inches, to keep out driving rain. Holes bored on an upward slant help to serve this purpose, also.

Ventilation should be provided by boring two or three augur holes through the side walls near the roof; this will allow heat to escape without making draughts, to which young birds are particularly susceptible. Or, a small opening could be left between the top of a side wall and the roof.

The inner walls of bird houses should be roughed or grooved, to help the young ones in learning to reach the entrance. As a general rule, bird houses should be placed rather low and not in dense woods, with the entrance turned away from prevailing winds.

Sheet-metal guards 18 inches in length placed around trunks of trees or poles at such a height as to prevent cats from springing from the ground and securing a foothold, will protect birds in houses from these enemies.

All bird houses should be repaired and thoroughly cleaned just before the nesting season comes. Periodical inspection of bird houses is essential after each brood has left. After cleaning the inside, the houses should be sprayed with cresol to destroy any pests that may have been overlooked.

In addition to planting trees, shrubs, and vines, and putting up water-proof roosting boxes, the providing of nesting material such as rags, ravelings, twine, excelsior, straw, hay, cotton, and hair, helps to attract birds. Food and water should also be supplied when not immediately available.

With a few exceptions, birds will more than pay for what little damage they may do.

TABLE 1.—*Dimensions and locations of bird houses*

Species	Floor of cavity, inches	Depth of cavity, inches	Entrance above floor, inches	Diameter of entrance, inches	Height above ground, feet	Location
Bluebirds	5 by 5	8	6	1½	5–10	Open sunlit orchards.
Robins	6 by 8	8	(1)	(1)	6–15	Shade trees or under eaves of shed or porch roof.
Chickadees	4 by 4	8–10	6–8	1⅛	6–15	Rustic homes in old orchards and borders of woodlands; suet and nut meats placed on trays in trees especially attract these birds.
Titmice	4 by 4	8–10	6–8	1¼	6–15	
Nuthatches	4 by 4	8–10	6–8	1¼	12–20	
House wrens	4 by 4	6–8	1–6	1	6–10	Shady or partly sunlit spots about door yards or orchards.
Bewick wrens	4 by 4	6–8	1–6	1	6–10	
Carolina wrens	4 by 4	6–8	1–6	1⅛	6–10	Borders of woodlands or in brushy areas.
Violet-green swallows	5 by 5	6	1–5	1½	10–15	Dead trees near bodies of water.
Tree swallows	5 by 5	6	1–5	1½	10–15	
Barn swallows	6 by 6	6	(1)	(1)	8–12	Shelves placed under eaves of building.
Purple martins	6 by 6	6	1	2½	15–20	On poles in open spaces near water.
Song sparrows	6 by 6	6	(2)	(2)	1–3	Covered shelves in thickets.
House finches	6 by 6	6	4	2	8–12	Shrubbery in orchards or dooryards.
Starlings	6 by 6	16–18	14–16	2	10–25	Old apple orchards.
Phœbes	6 by 6	6	(1)	(1)	8–12	Bridges or barns near bodies of water.
Crested flycatchers	6 by 6	8–10	6–8	2	8–20	Orchards, open woods, or in trees in pastures.
Flickers	7 by 7	16–18	14–16	2½	6–20	Above any immediately surrounding foliage.
Golden-fronted woodpeckers	6 by 6	12–15	9–12	2	12–20	
Red-headed woodpeckers	6 by 6	12–15	9–12	2	12–20	
Downy woodpeckers	4 by 4	8–10	6–8	1¼	6–20	
Hairy woodpeckers	6 by 6	12–15	9–12	1½	12–20	
Screech owls	8 by 8	12–15	9–12	3	10–30	Groves or apple orchards.
Saw-whet owl	6 by 6	10–12	8–10	2½	12–20	Trees in open groves.
Barn owls	10 by 18	15–18	4	6	12–18	Large trees or cupalos of buildings.
Wood ducks	10 by 18	10–15	3	6	4–20	Trunks of trees near shady streams.
Sparrow hawks	8 by 8	12–15	9–12	3	10–30	

[1] 1 or more sides open.   [2] All sides open.

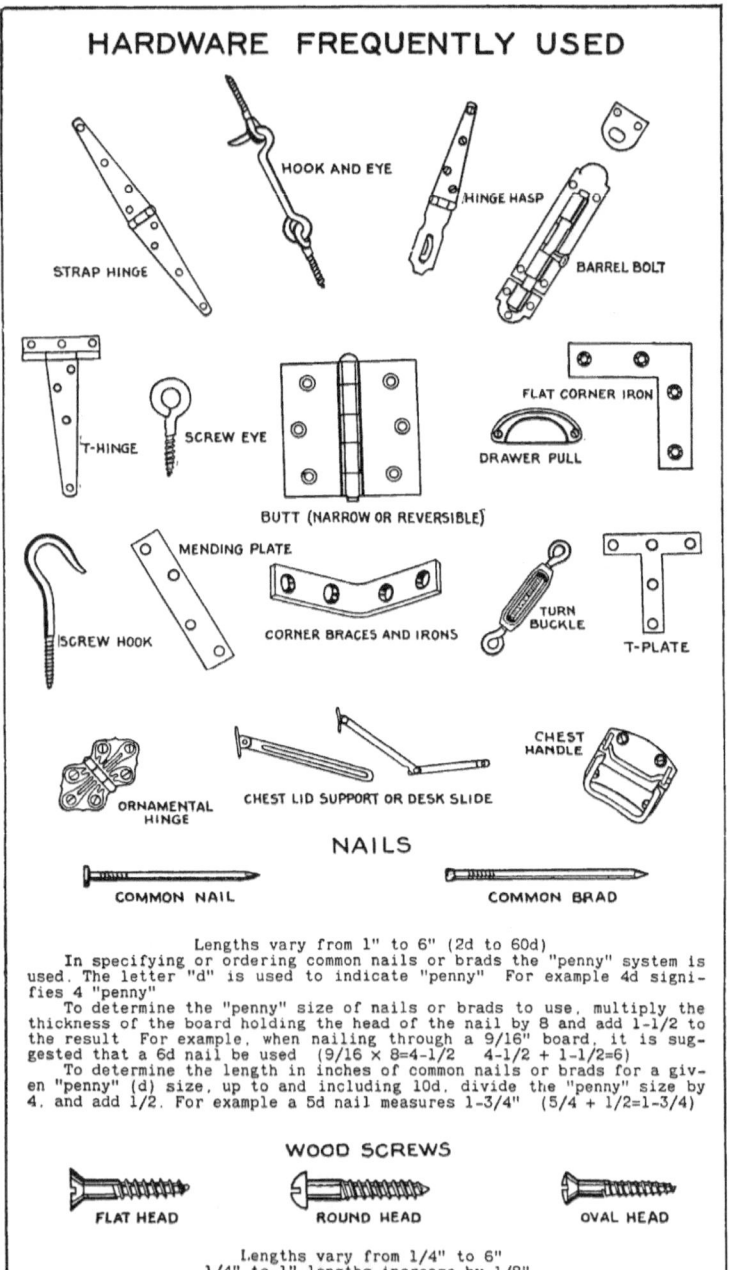

APPENDIX

COOPERAGE

WOODEN BARRELS

One of the first containers fashioned by man from the timber of the tree was the wooden barrel. The sides of the barrel are known as staves. These staves were hollowed from parts of the tree and jointed at the edges with a knife; together they made a complete circle. The staves were held together on the outside by hoops; the heads (top and bottom pieces) were rounded and fitted into the croze or groove of the staves. The completed result was called a barrel.

In the trade barrels are known as "tight" and "slack." Tight barrels are water-tight, holding liquids like oil, chemicals, kerosene, etc. Slack barrels are not water-tight. They are made to carry apples, potatoes, lime, and the like.

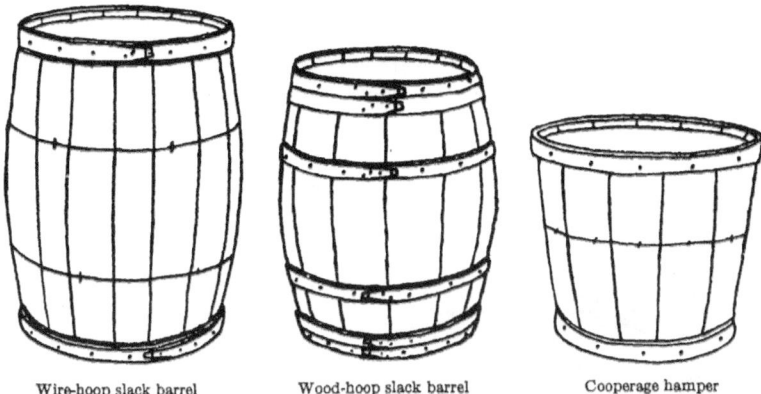

Wire-hoop slack barrel　　　Wood-hoop slack barrel　　　Cooperage hamper

Because tight barrels have a high resale value, very few, if any, are available without cost.

However, even though slack barrels also have a resale value, a great many may be collected from stores, dismantled, and made into other highly useful articles—bird houses, dog houses, chicken coops, fences, playhouses, old style hammocks, sled runners, flower tubs, skis, shingles for roofs of playhouses, sunroom furniture, etc.

The best method of dismantling a barrel is to knock off the hoops with a hammer, or, if there are any nails or fasteners, to extract them, and the whole barrel collapses. If it is desired to take out only one head, simply remove the top head, and if necessary, replace the hoops, which will hold the staves together.

FRUIT AND VEGETABLE PACKAGES

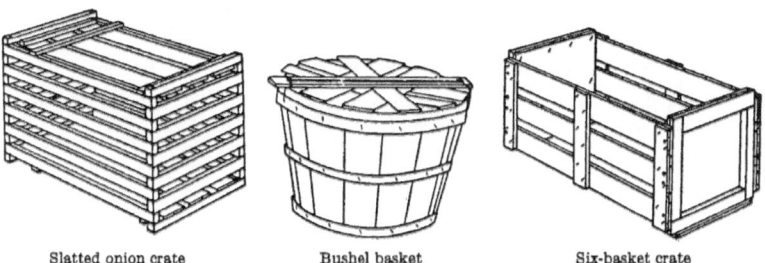

Slatted onion crate　　　Bushel basket　　　Six-basket crate

Secondhand fruit and vegetable packages are so readily available and of such desirable shape that they are always in demand for home and camp use. Wooden containers used for shipping these commodities may be separated into four classes;

namely, baskets, crates, boxes, and barrels. Among the most common types of fruit and vegetable packages now in use, are the 6-basket crate, bushel basket, and slatted onion crate shown above, and the orange box so familiar to everyone.

Orange boxes.—Two orange boxes are in common use—the Florida box and the California box. The main difference between the two boxes is in the ends. In the Florida box the ends and center partition are built up by nailing thin veneer to four head sticks. Solid pieces are used for the California box ends and center partition.

Six-basket crate.—The crate illustrated above measures 10½ by 11 by 24 inches; $1\frac{3}{16}$ by 1¼ inch material is used in the sticks forming the ends; $\frac{3}{16}$-inch veneer is used in the sides, top, and ends.

Bushel basket.—The bushel basket above is only one of many types of fruit and vegetable baskets. The wire handles on the basket make it especially useful for carrying things.

Slatted onion crate.—The bushel crate measures $11\frac{13}{16}$ by $12\frac{5}{16}$ by $20\frac{13}{16}$ inches. It is constructed of ½ by $1\frac{5}{16}$ inch hardwood slats held together with No. 12 gage wire. Directions for making handy camp stools from such crates are given in this booklet.

PLYWOOD BOXES MAKE USEFUL ARTICLES

Plywood boxes are made up of six panels, which form the ends, sides, top, and bottom. These panels are constructed by nailing sheets of plywood to cleats. Plywood used in box construction generally consists of three plies or sheets of lumber glued together. As the grain of the middle ply is placed at right angles to the outside plies, the plywood will not split. It provides excellent material for scroll-saw work, and for the construction of many of the articles illustrated in this booklet.

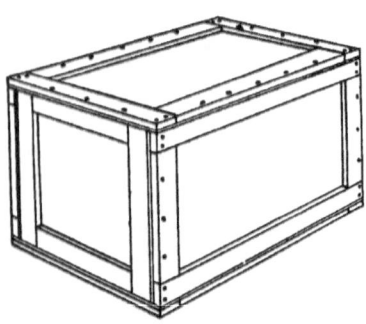

FIGURE 1.—Plywood box

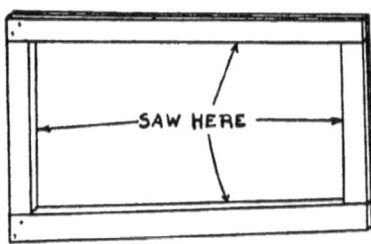

FIGURE 2.—Method of dismantling plywood box panel

Thickness of plywood used in box construction varies from $\frac{3}{32}$ to ¼ inch. Cross sections of cleats range from ⅝ by 1⅜ inches to $1\frac{3}{16}$ by 2 inches.

In order to remove the top from plywood boxes without damaging the panels, all nails holding the top to the sides and ends should be pulled. Nail pullers will be found useful in removing these nails. After the top is removed it is quite simple to knock the sides and bottom loose from the ends.

A panel may be dismantled by sawing, as shown in Figure 2, or if desired, by carefully withdrawing the staples holding the cleats to the plywood.

The panels may be used for ends and backs of furniture, and many uses can be found for the container intact.

NAILED WOODEN BOXES

APPROXIMATELY one billion nailed wooden boxes are manufactured each year in the United States — enough to distribute eight wooden boxes to each person in the country.

These boxes are still in good condition after they have been used, because they are built scientifically to be strong enough to deliver the goods packed in them without damage. It is wasteful to destroy used wooden boxes. There is good material in them for making the many useful articles described in this booklet, if one is careful not to split the boards when taking the boxes apart.

More than 15 per cent of all the timber cut annually in this country is made up in wooden boxes and crates; and yet, the manufacture of these shipping containers aids materially in the conservation of our forest resources. The nailed wooden box and crate industry utilizes the lower grades of lumber which are unavoidable by-products to the manufacture of construction and factory lumber. Much of it would be waste material if it could not be utilized in the manufacture of nailed wooden boxes and crates.

Since this lumber is of the lower grades with knots and blemishes in it, the box manufacturer is confronted with the problem of producing from it strong and efficient shipping containers that will protect merchandise in transit and carry it to the market in good, salable condition. He does this by cutting out the bad knots and blemishes that weaken the boards and by utilizing only the sound parts. The box manufacturers have the knack of getting every inch of usable lumber out of a board. The sawyers are given the dimensions of the pieces they are to make and can tell at a glance just how each board should be cut up to eliminate the bad parts and to leave the minimum amount of waste material.

A conservative estimate of the average amount of so-called "waste" material from a box factory is approximately 15 per cent. But this is not all wasted. Some of it is made into sawdust and shavings for commercial use. Some of it is sold for kindling wood, and some box manufacturers use it as fuel to supply power for their own plants.

In other words, a nailed wooden box manufacturer wastes no more of his lumber than a 10-year-old boy does of a stick of candy. The further utilization of the lumber in used wooden boxes in making useful articles is carrying the work of conserving our forests and utilizing forest products to an unusually high degree.

There are seven different styles of wooden boxes, the use of which has become so customary that they may be considered standard types.

Style 1 is without cleats and is employed chiefly for small boxes with light contents.

Style 2 has double-cleated ends and is particularly adapted for large boxes with heavy contents. The cleats and the double nailing of sides, top

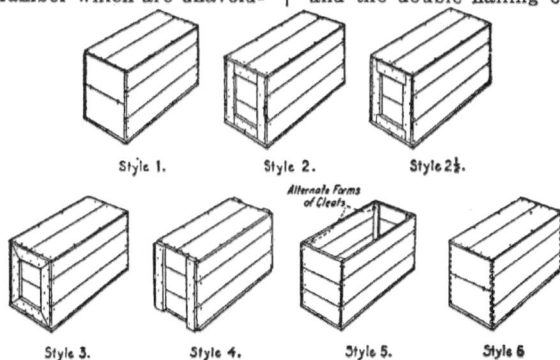

and bottom to both cleats and ends make this type of box unusually strong.

Style 2½ is similar to Style 2 except that the top and bottom cleats are set into side cleats, thus affording support when nailing.

Style 3 has mitered cleats.

Style 4 has single-cleated ends and is suitable for boxes of medium size and weight of contents. The sides have double rows of nailing in both cleats and ends, but the top and bottom have only a single row of nailing into the ends.

Style 5 is for boxes of medium size and weight of contents. It has interior cleats and is used to advantage for such articles as round cans and those having odd shapes which do not touch the corners of the case. Sometimes the width of the cleat is nailed to the side instead of to the end, and in other instances triangular or square cleats are nailed to both ends and sides.

Style 6 is a plain locked-corner box and is adapted for containers of small size and light weight of contents requiring rigidity.

HOW TO RECLAIM THE LUMBER IN WIREBOUND BOXES

A wirebound box is a light-weight, though very strong shipping container, whose sides, top and bottom are made from sheets of thin wood of the same thickness throughout, and fastened to a framework of heavier wood strips at the ends. Several steel wires pass completely around the body of the box. Each wire is firmly fastened to the thin wood by means of small staples, spaced at regular intervals and "clinched" on the inside. The binding wires serve not only to hold the top, sides and bottom together as one unit, but when the box is packed for shipment, it is closed, or sealed, by twisting the two ends of each wire together. The ends of a wirebound box are fastened to the framework of heavier wood strips by means of nails or staples. The thin wood with which a wirebound box is made is clear, free from knots. It is an excellent material for making any articles that call for the use of thin lumber. You will find it ideal for making many of the articles described in this and other "You Can Make It" books, such as bird-houses, airplane models, doll-houses, partitions for tool chests, drawers, etc., and various scroll-saw products.

Follow the instructions below for salvaging this useful material from discarded or used wirebound boxes:

Tools Needed.—All you need is a saw and a pair of nippers or wire-cutting pliers.

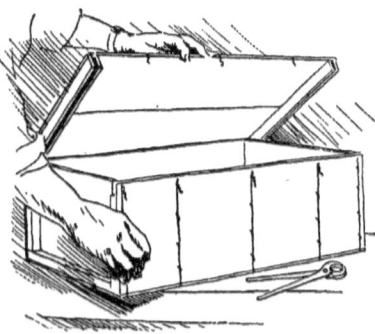

FIGURE 1.—*Typical Wirebound Box.*—Note the rows of wires stapled to the thin lumber.

First, fold back the lid of the box, as shown in Figure 1.

Next, remove the end panels, as shown in Figure 2. Make a cut with the saw just inside the two upright pieces of the framework to which the sides of the box are stapled. The cuts should extend down to, not *into*, the horizontal pieces to which the bottom of the box is stapled. The end panels should then be pushed in, so they will split away at the bottom. This will give you two pieces of usable thin wood.

Now, unfold the box, by bending the sides and lid down flush with the bottom. The result is a "mat", consisting of four sections, joined to each other by the wires. Turn the mat over, so that the wires and staples are uppermost, as shown in Figure 3.

FIGURE 2.—Removing the End Panels.

Next, cut the sections apart by clipping each binding wire where the sections are joined. This also is shown in Figure 3. The result is four separate sections of thin wood, each having several short lengths of wire stapled to it. Before you can use the wood, however, the staples and wires must be removed. To do this:

With nippers or pliers, pull out the staples in each section *except* those which hold the two outermost wires. Pull them out carefully, so as not to splinter the wood. The wires may be discarded.

FIGURE 3.—*Removing the Staples and Wires.*—Note that the two outermost wires are not removed.

Now, as shown in Figure 4, saw off the two outer edges of each section, about an inch inside the wires that were left attached to the wood. Discard these strips.

The sheets of thin wood you have thus obtained, together with the two end panels, are now ready for whatever use you may wish to put them, and they may be sawed or worked into any shape desired.

FIGURE 4.—*Cutting Away the Outside Edges.*—In circle—(1) A wirebound box, (2) The usable veneer pieces that came from it, and (3) The tools needed for the job.

AMERICAN LUMBER STANDARDS

The pieces specified in this booklet are given in accordance with American Lumber Standards for softwood lumber recommended by the Division of Simplified Practice of the United States Department of Commerce. Rough green lumber (not planed) as it comes from the mills nominally measures 1 by 3 inches, 1¼ by 4 inches, 1½ by 5 inches, etc. (thickness by width). However, in most cases boards purchased for making the various articles incorporated in this booklet should be dressed—that is, planed only on one side (S1S) or on two sides (S2S); the edges should also be dressed (S1E) or (S2E)—surfaced one and two edges, respectively.

This standard dressed lumber generally accepted throughout the country will have the following measurements:

Boards 1 inch thick (rough) will measure $25/32$ inch surfaced one side (S1S) or surfaced two sides (S2S). Other standard dressed thicknesses (S1S) or (S2S) measure, $11/16$, $9/16$, $7/16$, and $5/16$ inch.

Boards 3 inches wide (rough) measure ⅝ inches (S1E) or (S2E) surfaced one and two edges, respectively.

For the sake of convenience the following table, showing at a glance thicknesses and widths of dressed American Standard Lumber, with the corresponding rough-lumber measurements, is given:

TABLE 2.—*Dressed American Standard Lumber measurements*

Rough yard lumber	Dressed American Standard Lumber		
	Board thicknesses		Board widths, surfaced, S1E or S2E (inches)
	Resawed and surfaced, S1S or S2S (inch)	Surfaced, S1S or S2S (inches)	
Thickness (inches):			
1	$5/16$, $7/16$, $9/16$, $11/16$	$25/32$	
1¼		$1\,1/16$	
1½		$1\,5/16$	
1¾		$1\,7/16$	
2		$1\,5/8$	
Width (inches):			
3			2⅝
4			3⅝
5			4⅝
6			5⅝
7			6⅝
8			7½
9			8½
10			9½

BIBLIOGRAPHY

The following names of prominent publications dealing with wood-handicraft projects, in addition to those listed in You Can Make It, Volume I, are presented for the purpose of aiding those who may desire the names of publications dealing with camps and camping:

ADAMS, JOSEPH H.; Harper's Outdoor Book for Boys; Harper & Bros., New York, N. Y. 1907.
BEARD, D. C.; Do It Yourself; J. B. Lippincott Co., New York, N. Y. 1925.
BRIMMER, F. E.; Camp, Log Cabins, Lodges, and Clubhouses; D. Appleton & Co., New York, N. Y. 1925.
HOPKINS, R. T.; Every Boy's Open-Air Book. 1925.
KEPHART, H.; Camping and Woodcraft; The Macmillan Co., New York, N. Y. 1921.
JESSUP, E.; Roughing It Smoothly; G. P. Putnam's Sons, New York, N. Y. 1923.
MILLER, C. H.; Outdoor Sports and Games; Doubleday, Page & Co., Garden City, N. Y. 1911.
VERRILL, A. H.; The Boys' Outdoor Vacation Book; Dodd, Mead & Co., New York, N. Y. 1915.
Farm Home Conveniences, Farmers' Bulletin 927, United States Department of Agriculture, Washington, D. C.
Handicraft Club Work, Club Bulletin No. 11, extension division, Michigan Agricultural College, East Lansing, Mich.
Homes for Birds, Farmers' Bulletin No. 1456, United States Department of Agriculture, Washington, D. C.

INDEX

	Page
Adjustable book ends	25
Aquaplane	3
Auto jack	15
Barn owl house	6
Barrel stave hammock	11
Bathroom cabinet	37
Beach sandal	17
Bean-bag target	15
Bench	35
Bird feed box	9
Bird feeding house (revolving)	9
Bluebird house	5
Book and magazine rack	23
Bookcase seat	26
Bootery	21
Bootjack	38
Bracket	29
Breakfast table and cabinet	29
Broom holder	35
Brown-thrasher shelter	7
Canal boat	18
Canoe lazy back	3
Catbird shelter	7
Chair	29
Chickadee house	4
Clothes drier	34
Clotheshorse	34
Clothesline reel	17
Coat and hat rack	27
Correspondence holder	25
Dart target	15
Desk	25
Desk bookcase	23
Desk filing cabinet	29
Desk set	23
Door knocker	10
Drop-leaf table	27
Elevated wood box	33
Finch house	7
Fireplace wood basket	29
First aid box	37
Fishing pole rack	36
Fishing tackle box	4
Flicker house	6
Folding dressing table	21
Folding table	11
Folding table top	11
Foot scraper	17
Garden stick	10
Head mounting board	37
Hurdle	13

	Page
Iceless refrigerator	9
Kitchen table	35
Knife, fork, and spoon tray	32
Lighthouse	18
Linen closet	22
Live-bait box	3
Mail box	9
Meat or bread board	36
Necktie rack	38
Nuthatch house	4
Ore boat	18
Pan lid rack	33
Phœbe nest shelf	7
Portable tool box	37
Rabbit trap	4
Reading table	26
Robin shelter	7
Rocker	21
Safety match box holder	34
Salt box (animals)	17
Sawbuck	17
Sconce	29
Scow	20
Shelf	29
Shower	13
Sign	17
Song-sparrow shelter	7
Spring refrigerator	17
Steamboat	18
Stile	14
Stool	34
Swallownest shelf	7
Table horse	11
Tabouret	27
Tent peg	17
Titmouse house	4
Tool chest	36
Towel rack	33
Trash receptacle	33
Tugboat	20
Typewriter stand	25
Vanity	21
Vanity bench	21
Ventilator	22
Wall plate rack	35
Waste paper basket	23
Water turtle trap	4
Weather vane	11
Window flytrap	31
Window seat	29
Wren house	5

CONTENTS OF VOLUME I

	Page
Foreword	VI
General instructions	1
Sources of material	1
Tools	1
Preparing the material for use	1
Simple leg construction for box furniture	1
Decorating the finished article	2

	Page
Part I. Amusement devices	4–15
II. Equipment for the camp	16–25
III. Equipment for the garden	26–37
IV. Equipment for the home	38–49
Appendix (American Lumber Standards)	50
Bibliography	51
Index	52

ILLUSTRATIONS

Fig.	Page
1. Leg construction for box furniture	2
2. X-ray box	4
3. Reflectoscope	4
4. Sled	5
5. Submarine	6
6. Ski-skooter	6
7. Miniature Howe truss bridge	7
8. Skatemobile	7
9. Coaster	7
10. Baseball-equipment box	8
11. Home plate	9
12. Pitcher's plate	9
13. Water motor	9
14. Conveyor car	10
15–16. One-boy seesaw	10
17. Swing seat	10
18. Nested-box toss target	11
19. Kite reel	11
20. Ring toss target	11
21. Counter	12
22. Battleship	12
23. Target pistol	13
24. Silhouetteograph	14
25. Animal target box	14
26. Box kite	15
27. Game table	15
28. Camp kitchenette	16
29. Wall bookrack	16
30. Wall desk	17
31. Shavingette	17
32. Clock case and bookrack	17
33. Knife, fork, and spoon box	18
34. Corner shelf	18
35. Doorstop	19
36. Window stick	19
37. Utility box	19
38. Bench	20
39. Water-chute coaster	20
40. Butterfly and moth trap	21
41. Hanging lantern	21
42. Fishline reel	21
43. Box raft	22
44. Fishline drying reel	22
45. Fishing tip-up	22
46. Signal lantern	22
47. Live-bait box	23
48. Spreading board	23
49. Canoe lazyback	23
50. Herbarium press	23
51. Marine telescope	24
52. Salt box	24
53. Footstool	25

Fig.	Page
54. Germination flat	26
55. Germination-flat stand	26
56. Post trellis	26
57. Spotting board	27
58. Vegetable flat tamper	27
59. Vegetable flat marker	27
60. Folding trellis	28
61. Plant forcing box	28
62. Shrub label	28
63. Berry-box carrier	29
64. Bushel crate	29
65. Hand soil sieve	30
66. Poultry-feed bin	30
67. Brooder coop	31
68. Potting bench	31
69. Poultry green-feed box	32
70. Poultry drinking stand	33
71. Garden wheelbarrow	33
72. Beehive tool box	34
73. Concrete measuring box	34
74. Window plant box	34
75. Concrete wood float	35
76. Purple-martin house	35
77. Plumb board	36
78. Dog house	36
79. Portable tool box	37
80. Tool chest	38
81. Workbench	38
82. Miter board	39
83. Sawhorse	39
84. Laundry stick	40
85. Workshop utility cabinet	40
86. Waste-bag holder	40
87. Fireless cooker	41
88. Window refrigerator	42
89. Shoe box and seat	42
90. Folding bench ladder	43
91. Floor polisher	44
92. Shoe-blacking box	44
93. Whisk-broom holder	45
94. Letter rack	45
95. Serving tray	45
96. Sink rack	46
97. Knife stropper	46
98. Magazine or curio rack	46
99. Waste-paper basket	47
100. Odds and ends stand	47
101. Desk chair	47
102. Photographic enlarging apparatus	48
103. Hanging plant box	49
104. Sectional bookcase	49
105. Flour bin	49

www.ingramcontent.com/pod-product-compliance
Lightning Source LLC
Chambersburg PA
CBHW021132080526
44587CB00012B/1255